What the Citizen
Should Know About
THE NAVY

What the Citizen Should Know About
THE NAVY

— ★ —

HANSON W. BALDWIN

Illustrations by André Jandot

W. W. NORTON & COMPANY, INC.

PUBLISHERS · **NEW YORK**

Copyright, 1941, 1942, by

HANSON W. BALDWIN

First Published, March, 1941

Second and Revised Edition, January, 1942

PRINTED IN THE UNITED STATES OF AMERICA

CONTENTS

5

6   CONTENTS

LIST OF ILLUSTRATIONS

FOREWORD

WALTER LIPPMANN has called the United States Navy the "Weapon of Freedom." It is even more than that; upon its strength and capabilities may depend the destiny of the world.

For Sea Power has not lost its traditional influence upon history. The advent of Air Power has altered the design of men-of-war, modified tactical concepts, and limited and restricted surface ship operations, but the Kingdom of Blue Water is still the Kingdom of the Ship. Air Power—ship-borne and shore-based—has become an integral part of Sea Power; that fleet which does not project its might beyond the horizon by means of wings in the air is an obsolete one. But it is still the ship that is the chief carrier of trade and guardian of the sea lanes of the world; it is still the fighting ship that is our first line of defense.

Nothing that has occurred in the European War has invalidated that traditional concept of American defense. For it has been the silent strength of the British Fleet—keeping grim watch and ward upon the channel and the narrow seas, harrying Italian lines of communication in the Mediterranean, seizing advanced air and naval bases—that has been, together with Air Power, Albion's breastplate and buckler. Not that Sea Power

alone can win wars. The co-ordinate action of Sea
Power, Air Power, and Land Power supported by a
united people is the only receipt for victory. But to the
United States, separated by 3,000 miles of ocean from
Europe and 7,000 miles of sea from Asia, Sea Power
must be the fundament of defense.

Sea Power and all that it comprises are too often mis-
understood. For Sea Power can have no narrow meaning. First of all it is tradition—the tradition of great
waters, the traditions of great winds and lonely stars,
the tradition of the salt. Second, it is history—the history of men and ships, the personal history of a Scot
named Jones who fought in the fading twilight of a day
long gone, the still-unended history of a stout ship with
strakes like iron, the personal tragic history of a Lawrence who died with immortality upon his lips:

"Fight her till she sinks and don't give up the ship!"

But Sea Power is compact of the nation itself—not
only of its past but of its present. Fighting ships and
fighting men only epitomize the nation whose colors
they defend; they are a cross section of their country—
weathered and bent and shaped and disciplined to bear
the burden of responsibility. These men—the lives they
lead, their training, their ratings, and their ranks;
these ships—their types, their purposes, and the many
other diverse elements that blend to comprise Sea
Power are but little known and little understood.

This book attempts no definitive analysis of their
character; it tries, rather, to tell in simple, homely language what Sea Power is and to describe the different

types of fighting ships, the ranks and ratings of the
men who man them. This is a reportorial handbook for
Mr. Jones of Omaha who may never have seen the sea;
the specialist and the savant will find no cultured
studies within these pages; here is merely a simple exposition of what the average citizen might want to know
about the Navy. And for those who do not understand
the language of the sea, a glossary of nautical and naval
terms is included. If this book serves to define Sea Power
and to explain, in layman's language, the United States
Navy, it will have accomplished its purpose.

H. W. B.

January, 1941

CHAPTER ONE

———

ELEMENTS OF SEA POWER

THE elements of modern Sea Power are as diffuse and diverse and astonishing as the mind of man. Sea Power comprehends most of scientific knowledge; it enlists in its service men of every class, race, and creed; it taps for its sustenance mine and mountain, forest and factory, and farm. Its sole common denominator is the sea; out of the earth and from the nation it draws men and matériel to the salt, there to be shaped and fashioned, broken or gentled, tamed and taught.

Sea Power comprises far more than fighting ships and the crews to man them; its elements are almost as various as the sailor's wardrobe of 1790. A sign of that date in Portsmouth, England, so Commander Leland P. Lovette, U.S.N. has discovered, read:

MORGAN, MERCER AND SEA DRAPER

Sailors rigged complete from stem to stern, viz.: Chapeau, napeau, flying jib and flesh bag, inner pea, outer pea and cold defender; rudder case and service to the same; up haulers and down traders, foreshoes, lacings, gaskets, etc.

The "lacings," "gaskets," "flying jibs," and "flesh bags" are gone with the wind, but Sea Power today is

even more complex than in the days of sail. Lignum
vitae (or cutless rubber) from tropical jungles (for bearings for propeller shafts), oil from the wells of Oklahoma, steel from Pittsburgh's mills, silk (for powder
bags) from Japan—these are only a few of the products
which go into a single ship. And fighting ships are only
one of the elements of Sea Power.

Those elements have been variously defined, but all
authorities, from Alfred Thayer Mahan, the great
apostle of Sea Power, to contemporary writers like Admiral Sir Herbert Richmond, agree that Sea Power includes fighting ships, merchant ships, and bases. To this
triumvirate it is now immediately necessary to add a
fourth element—air power. Nor does this conclude the
long roll. Broken down into basic elements Sea Power
means: geography (a seacoast); fighting ships of all categories from battleships to motor torpedo boats; auxiliaries such as supply ships, transports, tankers, and hospital ships; merchantmen of all types; officers and men
to man the ships; bases with drydocks, wharves, machine
shops, airfields, ramps, anchorages, barracks, fuel tanks
to build the ships and their planes, to repair them, overhaul them, and fuel them; machinists and skilled labor
to perform all these services; planes of all types to take
off from the flat decks of carriers, to be hurled from
catapults, to leap from the back of a crested roller; pilots and trained crews to fly the planes; training schools
for officers and men; and finally, a vast complex of industrial establishments, steel mills, ordnance plants,
plane factories, raw material resources, money and people.

Sea Power is thus an expression of a nation's strength; only a great industrial nation can support great Sea Power; a navy is an expensive and intricate arm; even such an advanced country as Canada has no facilities for building a battleship, or even a cruiser.

Sea Power finds its roots in many causes. Admiral Sir Herbert Richmond declares in his book, *Sea Power and the Modern World,* either "its origin is due to an intrinsic need arising out of an inability either to find a livelihood for a people or to be secure against the domination of others; or it is due to a desire to conquer or to enforce the will of the state upon others."

Mahan, however, limits its origins more closely:

"The ships (merchant ships) that thus sail to and fro," he writes in his *Influence of Sea Power Upon History,* must "have secure ports to which to return, and must, as far as possible, be followed by the protection of their country throughout the voyage. This protection in time of war must be extended by armed protection. The necessity of a navy, in a restricted sense of the word, springs, therefore, from the existence of a peaceful shipping, and disappears with it, except in the case of a nation which has aggressive tendencies, and keeps up a navy merely as a branch of the military establishment."

Mahan's exposition, while in some way true, is an oversimplification of the facts of history. Switzerland, without a seacoast, obviously has no need of Sea Power. But in the heyday of the clipper ship, when this nation's international commerce was at a peak, our fighting fleet was at a nadir. Before the present war the Scandinavian States, which carried a large share of the world's trade in the bottoms of their numerous merchant ships, had neither the money and facilities nor, so they thought, the need for real navies. For navies, it must be realized, are expensive and nonproductive institutions; unlike merchant ships, fighting ships do not earn their way but eat up government funds and increase taxes. They can be justified only, therefore, as a form of insurance: (1) to protect merchant shipping, and/or (2) to protect a nation or an area against possible aggression; or as a form of speculation to further aggressive expansion.

There is, however, still a further reason for Sea Power: as an implementation of diplomacy, and as a necessary part of the accouterments of a great power. There is no great power in the world today that is not also a considerable Sea Power. Russia, which has the weakest navy of the larger Sea Powers, is probably also the weakest, inherently, of those powers; certainly her industrial establishment is the least able of them all to manufacture such tremendous items as 16-inch gun-liners, intricate breechblocks, 18-inch-thick slabs of case-hardened, carbonized, nickel steel armor; certainly Russia, with her great undeveloped, underpopulated open spaces, is an introvert rather than an extrovert nation, and thus has less use for Sea Power than any of her contemporaries. In the modern world of power politics and political change, in the modern world where all nations live dangerously, and none can tell "from what red hell" tomorrow may spring, the necessity of navies seems obvious.

Yet it is necessary to labor the point further in order that a clear understanding of the elements of American

Sea Power and their interrelationship, each to each, be gained.

The economic, political, psychological, and historical conditions from which Sea Power develops are an integral part of history; in the events of yesterday and the facts of today man has found sound reasons for constructing fighting ships. Those reasons, we have seen, are primarily three: aggressive conquest; defensive protection; the protection of trade.

In the Spanish-American War, and earlier in the Mexican War, the United States Navy was utilized as one of the implements of conquest, but today our era of "Manifest Destiny" and imperial expansion has probably ended; the American Navy of the 20th century is universally regarded by our people as a shield of defense and a powerful stabilizing factor in the ancient world-wide game of power politics. We covet no foreign soil; we have no desire, and above all, there is no compelling reason, such as the slow, inexorable pressure of overpopulation, or the driving whiplash of economics, for overseas expansion.

Moreover, our foreign trade, though important to our capitalistic system of free enterprise which is built upon the exploitation of new markets, is not completely indispensable to the nation. It is an asset and one to be guarded, but it represents only 7 to 10 per cent of our total production, our domestic markets absorbing the greater part of our manufactured and agricultural products.

American Sea Power, therefore, is not the by-product of foreign trade, nor is it the result of expansionist policies. Our Navy's role as guardian of our merchant marine and our overseas trade is an important one, but it is not the primary one. The United States Navy is America's first line of defense; its ships and planes are rapidly becoming the outer ramparts of the entire Western Hemisphere. It is a Navy for defense; that is the meaning of our Sea Power.

But we must examine more closely what sea *defense* means. A navy cannot hold a rigid line as can a land army. Sea Power is mostly composed of things that move —men and ships. It can have no static definition; mobility is the keynote of power on the seas. A navy for defense, if that navy is to endure, cannot mean a navy leashed to its own bases, a navy that does not venture into enemy waters. We have no aggressive, expansionist intentions in the Western Pacific; we want no slice of China. But suppose Japan—a nation which has expansionist policies as her modern history shows—should seize the American Philippines. We could not regain those islands by defensive measures, by holding our fleet in Hawaii and the Pacific Coast bases, by fighting at sea only if Japan sent her ships to Hawaii or the West Coast. Obviously, if we wanted to defeat Japan, if we wanted to retake the Philippines, our fleet would have to take *offensive* action; it would have to throw some sort of a blockade around the Japanese Islands, and/or it would have to push into the Western Pacific in order to force the Japanese Fleet to come out and give combat. This is a good example of how the *defensive* navy of a nation that has no imperialist ambitions would be

used offensively, used in the only way in which Sea
Power can mean success.

Still another example will show the necessity of far-
ranging action by Sea Power. Most of our supplies of
rubber and tin now come from the Far East. If we wish
to continue the importation of those vital raw materials
during wartime, merchant ships must carry them from
the Far East to our shores, and those merchant ships
must be guarded against enemy attack. Ships cannot operate indefinitely over tremendous sea distances without
refueling, and that means bases, another of the obvious
elements of Sea Power.

Consider these two examples together. A blockade of
Japan, which we might have to undertake if Japan
seized the Philippines, means interception or severance
of the sea routes to Japan. But if we are not able to
guard effectively our own Far Eastern sea routes over
which flow those vital supplies of rubber and tin, then
Japan may sever them. Thus, it becomes clear that the
functions of navies—which it must be remembered are
only one of the elements of Sea Power—are to dominate
sea communications, to dominate the wide waters of
the oceans. The very immensity of those waters and the
great distances of certain markets and raw materials
from the homeland complicate the problem of Sea
Power, nor can navies accomplish their purpose by dominating the *surface* alone. Obviously, as the German
submarine and air campaigns have shown, navies of today must be prepared to exercise control, not only of the
surface of blue water, but also must extend their power
to the empyrean blue *above,* and to the dismal depths

below. Naval war, therefore, has become a three-dimensional problem, and the elements of Sea Power, complex enough in the days of the wind ships, have now become legion.

The purposes of, and reasons for, American Sea Power are thus clearly evident. We need a certain amount of Sea Power (merchant ships protected by fighting ships and fighting planes operating from well-located bases) to take our exports to overseas markets and to bring back those raw materials, such as rubber and tin, which cannot be procured in their natural state within the continental borders of this country. But more emphatically, we need Sea Power to prevent any hostile nation from dominating the seas and using them as it wishes—perhaps for transporting an army to the Western Hemisphere, perhaps for clamping a close blockade around our coasts, perhaps for raiding our cities with planes from carrier decks. We need a navy for defensive purposes, but, as we have seen, if it is to be used successfully it must be used offensively.

Today, politically, economically, and strategically the United States is assuming the position in world affairs so long held by England. England is an insular power, an island empire, whose greatness has been solidly based on the domination of the British Fleet over world sea communications. Today, because of the shrinkage of time and space due to modern transport and communication developments (the plane, the telephone, the radio), England is virtually no longer an island but a part of the continent of Europe; her security can no longer be based upon Sea Power alone. But the United

States, far from war-torn Europe and Asia, has, in a sense, become an insular power, separated by still-wide spaces of ocean from potential enemies. For us Sea Power still has its traditional validity; for us Sea Power is still our first line of defense.

The new naval policy of the nation, approved by the Secretary of the Navy as of September 14, 1940, inferentially recognizes these principles:

FUNDAMENTAL POLICY

To maintain the Navy in strength and readiness to uphold national policies and interests, and to guard the United States and its continental and overseas possessions.

GENERAL POLICIES

1 To develop the Navy to a maximum in fighting strength and ability to control the sea in defense of the nation and its interests.

2 To make effectiveness in war the objective of all development and training.

3 To organize and maintain the Navy for major operations in both the Atlantic and Pacific oceans.

4 To maintain and develop naval aviation as an integral part of the naval forces.

5 To maintain the Marine Corps in such strength as to provide the requisite fleet marine force and detachments for other naval purposes.

6 To develop and maintain shore activities, including

bases suitably located and defended, for the support of
the mobile forces.

7 To locate shore activities in such geographical areas
and construct them in such sites and in such manner as
will promote security against air and other attack; and
to apply this policy to existing activities as practicable.

8 To advance the art of naval warfare and to promote
the development of naval matériel.

9 To maintain and train the officer and enlisted personnel requisite for the regular establishment and to provide for the procurement and training of the personnel
required for the expanded war organization.

10 To plan the procurement of matériel to meet wartime needs and to foster civil industries and activities
useful in war.

11 To exercise economy in expenditures as compatible
with efficiency.

12 To make systematic inspections of naval activities and
matériel.

13 To encourage the growth of the merchant marine and
of commercial aviation.

14 To co-operate fully with other departments and
agencies of the government.

Sea Power, it is thus evident, is composed of far more
than tons and guns. It is one of the most complex of
human institutions, but its essential elements, as we
have seen (each element will be treated at greater length
later in this book), are men and officers, fighting ships,
auxiliaries and merchantmen, and bases.

Men and officers—the soul and spirit and primal force
of any Sea Power—today are numbered in the hundreds

of thousands in the American Navy and are steadily increasing in number as the Navy expands. As of October
1, 1941, there were:

219,195	Enlisted Men (Regular Navy)
2,600	Enlisted Men (Retired, Recalled to Active Duty)
49,373	Enlisted Men (Reserves on Active Duty)
47,027	Enlisted Marines (Regular)
11,491	Enlisted Marines (Reserves on Active Duty)
11,830	Officers (Regular Navy)
19,834	Officers (Reserves on Active Duty, Navy)
1,486	Officers (Retired, Recalled to Active Duty, Navy)
2,026	Marine Officers (Regular)
1,767	Marine Officers (Reserves on Active Duty)

TOTAL 366,629

These figures are changing daily as the nation's greatest naval expansion program since the World War pro-
gresses. The exact objectives in man power are not yet
certain, but the tentative goals compared with 1940
strengths are:

JUNE 30, 1940		1945–46
145,000	Men	} 675,000
13,162	Officers	
25,000	Marines	} 112,000
1,568	Marine officers	
119,332	Civilians	—— ?

Ships, the second element of Sea Power, the United States numbers in the thousands. As of the fiscal year 1940, the Navy operated a total of 653 commissioned vessels (exclusive of the Coast Guard) of all types, from battleships to harbor tugs and small craft. Three hundred and forty of these were combatant vessels; the remainder were auxiliaries of all types, from submarine rescue vessels to destroyer tenders and small craft.

The merchant shipping of the nation (as of September 30, 1940) consisted of the following principal elements:

Ocean-going ships of	NUMBER	TONNAGE
1,000 tons and over......	377	2,345,185
Coastal Shipping	699	4,024,769
Ships under repair	99	466,279
Ships laid up	63	401,393
TOTAL	1,238	7,237,626

The grand total of all ships of 100 tons or more—both seagoing and Great Lakes—was 3,270 vessels of 11,874,384 tons.

A vast ship construction program, which started on a modest scale soon after President Roosevelt took office, gathered momentum in 1936 and was progressing at high speed by 1941. Every single shipway in the country was occupied by the keel of a seagoing vessel —man-of-war or merchantman—and contracts for many additional ways and vessels had been let.

The naval shipbuilding program, its objective the creation of a "two-ocean navy" (a navy twice the size of the present one which will be able to maintain strong combatant fleets in both oceans, Atlantic and Pacific, simultaneously), was the greatest in the country's history. Three hundred and sixty-eight combatant ships were under construction in the beginning of 1941, in addition to seventy-five naval auxiliaries. About 143 merchant ships, tankers, yachts, tugs, and miscellaneous craft had been purchased by the Navy during the summer and fall of 1940 to add to its existing fleet of auxiliaries. And the Merchant Marine of the nation, under the guidance of the Maritime Commission, headed by Rear Admiral Emory S. Land, U.S.N. (Retired), was engaged in the greatest merchant shipbuilding program in all history with 1,383 vessels totaling 13,500,000 deadweight tons, building or planned. Most of these were scheduled for completion by the end of 1943.

The objectives:

Navy

TYPE	1941	1946 ?
Battleships	17	32
Aircraft Carriers	6	18
Cruisers	37	91
Destroyers	159	364
Submarines	105	185
TOTAL	324	690 (3,487,700 tons)

Merchant Marine

	1940	1943
Merchant Vessels of all types over 1,000 tons..	1,238	2,500 ?

The Navy's flying fleets were similarly expanding during 1940.

	OCTOBER 1, 1941	1942 ?	1946 ?
Planes	4,535	10,000	15,000

Behind the fighting elements of Sea Power is ranged a vast complex of shore activities. The United States and its outlying possessions are divided into sixteen naval districts, with some twelve navy yards, twenty ordnance establishments; four engineering plants, and a total of more than 40 operating bases, air bases or stations, naval stations, and naval activities of various sorts throughout the continental United States, in Alaska and the Aleutians, in the Atlantic Islands from Newfoundland to Trinidad, at Panama, in mid-Pacific, and as far west as the Philippines.

And behind these essential elements of Sea Power—men, ships of the sea and the sky, and bases—are the machines and men of industry, the forges and the foundries of Pittsburgh, a steel industry with the world's greatest capacity (some 85,000,000 tons annually), an oil industry that supplies the roaring burners of our fleet and the needs of most of the world, a nation of 131,-000,000 people whose future may rest upon the seas. It is a nation with proud traditions of industrial greatness, a nation that at Armistice, 1918, had 1,284 launching ways, more than double those of all the rest of the world combined, a nation that laid keels at Hog Island during the World War era one every five and a half days, a nation which built destroyers and Eagle boats like Ford cars, a nation which has constructed in one year more tons of shipping than any other nation in world history, and a nation which can do the same again!

Thus American Sea Power, with proud traditions of past greatness behind it, is today expanding to unprecedented strength. Today the fighting fleet is equal to any in the world; the merchant fleet is second only to Britain; tomorrow American Sea Power may reach unprecedented and unchallenged strength. But its elements of greatness, then as now, will be men and ships and bases—but the greatest of these is men.

CHAPTER TWO

THE ENLISTED MAN

IN THE days of the windships, with their "Long Toms" and carronades; in the days when the frigate *Constitution* wrote imperishable history with the battle smoke and flaming thunder of her guns, a man-o'-warsman was rough, tough, and ready; he was "begotten in the galley and born under a gun; every hair a rope yarn, every tooth a marlinespike; every finger a fishhook, and in his blood right good Stockholm tar."

The sailor of our early Navy was a rollicking customer—hard-swearing, hard-drinking, hard-living, hard-fighting; his back was scarred with the livid welts of the "cat"; he lived on salt pork and ship's biscuit; wounded in a fight, the surgeon and his mates strapped him to a table and gave him a leather gag to chew on while they sawed off his leg. He slept in a hammock, and when he died he was sewed up in a hammock with a brace of round shot at his feet, the last stitch through his nose for luck, and he was given a proper deep-sea burial with the sough of the wind and the rataplan of the blocks as his threnody, and with Davy Jones awaitin' to receive him down below.

The bluejacket was a man of iron then, fighting wooden ships; he was a man of muscle, and had to be to manhandle the guns, to haul on the braces, and to walk the capstan 'round. He had little education and little use for it; "X—His Mark" was frequently affixed to the ship's papers of the period.

The bluejacket today is altogether a different breed. He shares several qualities in common with his strong-backed, boisterous forebear. He is still a seaman, loving the salt. He serves his country now as then. And the young bluejacket of today is linked with those men of a century and more ago by the strong ties of tradition.

But the sailor today is a typical young American, drawn to the sea from the farms of Iowa, the great forests of the Northwest, the cities and factories of the East, the cotton fields and cane lands of the South. He uses his brain more than his brawn. He is well-educated; the average recruit has had almost three years of high school. He has a vast fund of common sense; he has to possess that too rare quality; if he doesn't have it when he enters it is quickly knocked into him in the practical workshop of the sea. He is healthy; he has to be.

Today the bluejacket (he doesn't much like the slang term "gob" given him during the World War) must run machines with brain power, not reef sails with muscle power. Machines that do everything but think. Machines that calculate and integrate and solve problems. Machines that propel ships. He must control powerful forces, frightening forces—steam at 500 pounds pressure per square inch, steam so scaldingly hot that it cannot be seen, but an old broom held over a tiny leak in a steampipe will suddenly flare into flame!

The modern mariner, therefore, must have considerable "savvy." But he is still a sailor, and he likes to be called one: "Hi-ya, sailor!" is one good seaman's typical salutation to another—cocky, assertive, confident, indicating pride of his profession, of the blues he wears, of the Navy and the country he serves.

The men who man the Navy come from every state and from many other places besides. More than 135,000 of them (as of June, 1940) were native-born, and the average recruit is the son of native-born parents. Five hundred and fifty came from Guam; eighty-five from Samoa; 1,582 from the Philippines, and three from the Virgin Islands—America's outposts. A great, great number come from the farm states, far from the tang of the salt, though New York, with the largest population of any of the forty-eight states, with 7,766 representatives in the Navy, exceeded any other state in the Navy of 1940.

There are representatives of many of the world's races in the Navy; almost 133,000 of the Navy's seamen—by far the overwhelming proportion—are white. But there are more than 4,000 Negroes who, since the passage of the Philippine Independence Act, have been enlisted to serve as officers' mess attendants in place of Filipinos. But there are still many Filipinos in the service, a few of them born in the United States, others who were serving in the Navy when the order banning further initial enlistments of native Filipinos was promulgated. There are Chamorros, Hawaiians, sixteen American Indians, and even some Chinese, some of them citizens of this melting pot that is America, others vestigial remnants of the old Navy—the Navy that used to hire stewards on the China station in the old days and utilize their culinary capabilities in an entirely unofficial capacity.

Such a picturesque and wonderful old fellow was Tip, Chinese officers' steward par excellence, his smiling yellow face belying his years of service, his original status as "Number 1" boy on a China gunboat, now regularized with a uniform and the stripes of long service. Tip was noted for his cooking prowess; he was a wizard with the pots and pans, and in purchasing native delectables for the officers' mess he made a dollar or a peso or a mark go a long way. But he had one fault; in very rare intervals he used to like to look upon the wine when it was red. He was captain's steward for years, an exalted and high-ranking position in his own opinion, and in that of his companions in the galleys and storerooms, but he fell from his high place. Once, in Cherbourg, France, the captain ordered a sumptuous dinner with all the trimmings for a most special party of guests; the captain gave Tip some of his own money, telling him to go ashore and get everything he needed. The dinner hour came and there was no dinner; as the captain fumed the ship's boat pulled alongside, and Tip, triumphant and solemnly grave, marched with Oriental dignity into the sanctum sanctorum bearing a broken French ice-cream freezer and two eggs!

The young man who wants to enlist in the Navy must apply at a Navy Recruiting Station in his home community. The recruiting posters—"Join the Navy and See the World," now altered to the more important obligation, "Join the Navy and Serve Your Country"

—will tell him where to go, or the police or local civic officials will know.

If he has never been in the Navy before the recruit must be:

Native-born of fully naturalized citizens of the U. S.

Not less than 18 years of age when enlisted.

Under 31 years of age when enlisted, except that ex-members of the Marine Corps, Army, and Coast Guard with creditable discharges may be enlisted beyond this age, provided they are under 35 years of age.

Of good character.

Mentally qualified.

Not less than 64 inches in height (the Navy may be willing to waive this requirement if you come within an inch of it).

Of proportionate weight to age and height.

If he doesn't meet these general requirements the young man will not be accepted. If he does, then he will be "put through the works."

Enlistment requirements in the Marine Corps, which is a part of the Navy, are somewhat different. A marine "must be something of a sailor and everything of a soldier," as the Corps' "prospectus" says. "In addition to taking on quite a bit of seamanship, the leatherneck learns to hike like an infantryman, and handle guns like an artilleryman. He learns something of wireless telegraphy, mechanics, and aviation."

Marine Corps enlistments are for a period of four years. The applicant must be between 18 and 25, except that a few men between 25 and 30 "with outstanding qualifications" may be accepted. The height range is

64 to 72 inches; married men are not accepted. Physical and character examinations are rigid; the Marine Corps is a corps d'élite, small but proud; the applicant must be prepared for stiff discipline, and he must be ready for fighting and hard duty anywhere from "the halls of Montezuma to the shores of Tripoli," as the Marines' song goes. If he can meet all these qualifications the potential marine, like the potential navy recruit, will be "put through the works."

"The works" include a rigid physical examination, an intelligence test, and various references. The applicant must furnish a birth certificate or other evidence of his age, the written consent of his parent or guardian if he is under 21 years of age; he must furnish references from two responsible persons or a list of former employers or school teachers. The applicant must have no police record and no juvenile record, except for minor infractions, such as parking on the wrong side of the street, which do not involve what the Navy and the law ominously call "moral turpitude." He is finger-printed, blood-typed, and given the Kahn reaction and other laboratory tests. The fingerprints eventually go to the Federal Bureau of Investigation for checking against the millions in their files. The Navy is "choosey" about its recruits; it wants no criminals or men of bad character; the old saw about sending a boy into the Navy to reform him is not popular with the Navy; the fleet is not a reform school.

With all this behind him, the applicant is then usually placed on a waiting list. After a period which may vary from a few days to a few weeks, depending in part upon

the need of the fleet for men, the young applicant reports back to the Navy Recruiting Station, signs the
"Shipping Articles," and with right hand raised, he is
sworn in:

"I do solemnly swear that I will bear true faith and
allegiance to the United States of America, and that I
will serve them faithfully and honestly against all their
enemies whatsoever, and that I will obey the orders of
the President of the United States, and the orders of
the officers appointed over me, according to the rules
and articles for the government of the Navy."

The recruit is now officially a "boot" (Navy equivalent for "rookie") in the United States Navy, with the
rating of apprentice seaman, with a monthly pay of $21,
and six years of naval service on any ship in any clime
ahead of him. (The Navy will not accept any of the nation's one-year drafted men; it requires far more than a
year to train a landsman how to handle the complex instruments of naval war.)

He is handed a little booklet, *Helpful Hints to the
Navy Recruit,* and the first paragraph is immediately
impressive:

"You are now beginning your naval career. You are
entering an honorable service, a service with a splendid
history. Let it be a matter of pride with you to do your
part in upholding the good name and traditions of the
service. Obedience is of first importance and absolutely
necessary in the Navy. Orders must be obeyed promptly
and without argument or question, whether given by
an officer, petty officer, or non-rated man in charge of
others."

The recruit is sent to one of four naval training stations in the United States: Newport, Rhode Island; Great Lakes, Illinois; Norfolk, Virginia; or San Diego, California (or to Parris Island, or to San Diego, if he has enlisted in the Marines).

Here the recruit for the first time changes from civilian clothes to uniform. His civilian clothes, and articles which are not allowed, such as cameras, are sent home by insured express, and the boot draws at Uncle Sam's expense his outfit of issue clothing—a hammock, complete with its clews, mattress, blankets, and lashings; white canvas sea bag for his clothing; the traditional blue and white uniforms of the Navy—with bell-bottomed trousers, tight at the hips, wide-flaring at the bottom to permit the sailor to roll them up above the knees when scrubbing decks or landing through the surf. The first outfit costs complete more than $100; the boot stencils his name upon each article carefully, for hereafter throughout the rest of his naval career replacements or additions to the sailor's wardrobe are made at the sailor's own expense.

The boot is then plunged into an exacting and precise routine of discipline—school of the recruit, manual of arms, school of the squad, setting-up exercises, semaphore signals, physical drill under arms, boats, bag inspection, all of which keeps him busy daily from 5.45 A.M. to 4.45 P.M. He must learn, first of all, personal cleanliness; he may find later that if he doesn't keep himself and his belongings clean aboard ship his shipmates may give him a "sand-and-canvas"—a rough scrubbing with sand and canvas under a deck hose sluicing

salt water. He learns naval nomenclature; he learns how
the Navy tells time by the ship's bell; he finds out that
each new day begins at midnight or "0000"; and the
cycle of hours continues through the day, somewhat
after the European fashion, past "1200" which is noon,
and so on through the afternoon ("1300" is one P.M.;
"1630" is four-thirty P.M.) to midnight which is "2400."

The bells keep pace with this formula, but repeat
themselves as follows:

TIME

BELLS	A.M.				P.M.	
1 bell	0030	0430	0830	1230	1630	2030
2 bells....	0100	0500	0900	1300	1700	2100
3 bells....	0130	0530	0930	1330	1730	2130
4 bells....	0200	0600	1000	1400	1800	2200
5 bells....	0230	0630	1030	1430	1830	2230
6 bells....	0300	0700	1100	1500	1900	2300
7 bells....	0330	0730	1130	1530	1930	2330
8 bells....	0400	0800	1200	1600	2000	2400

An easy way to remember this system is that the day
starts at midnight with eight bells. At 12.30 A.M. one bell
is struck; at 1 A.M., two bells; and one bell is added for
each half hour of passing time until eight bells is
reached, when the cycle is started all over again. Eight
bells are struck, therefore, every four hours of the day
and night.

The normal period of recruit training at the naval
training stations is twelve weeks; this has been reduced
during the present emergency first to eight weeks, then
to six weeks.

The capacity of the stations also has been and is being materially increased. The annual capacity of our four training stations will total about 175,000 as of February 1, 1942. Norfolk will handle 40,000; Newport, 38,000; San Diego, 43,000; and Great Lakes, 54,000.

The rookie, still wearing on both cuffs of the sleeves of his blue uniform jumper the single thin horizontal white stripe which designates him as an apprentice seaman, leaves the training stations with a fundamental knowledge of discipline and hygiene, with some knowledge of naval nomenclature, seamanship, communications, gunnery, etc., and with a great excitement and anticipation in his heart.

He does not know where he is going until he receives his orders—a draft of so many men to this or that ship or station. And then his seagoing career starts.

The boot moves into a strange new world—the world of wind and water, the world of the ship. In it he finds himself a "hayseed," a landsman, a novitiate, green to the salt. His life is behind him; his life is before him.

He stands in line (he has already found that much of life in the Navy is standing in line), and passes his hammock, lashed with its seven hitches, his own sea bag and those of his fellow boots up the gangway. He waits. His service record which will be his official "shadow" in the files of the Navy until the day he dies, his pay accounts, and transfer papers are turned over to the executive officer of the ship, who, as his title implies, is second-in-command and "general manager" of the vessel. The executive officer assigns the boots to divisions;

often, if a large draft reports aboard simultaneously, the new men may be organized in an "X Division" for a month or so. The "X Division" is a school division, consisting entirely of apprentice seamen who are trained by petty officers and officers in the customs, habits, and routine of life afloat.

The apprentice seaman will find himself a name and a number on his ship's and division's watch, quarter, and station bill. "Jimmy legs," or the ship's omnipotent master-at-arms, who keeps the keys to the brig and who sees and knows "all that is evil done" may take him in hand for a talk-to or a bit of friendly advice. In any case the youngster will soon find his billet. It may be only a couple of hammock hooks depending from the I beams in the cork-pebbled steel overhead, above the mess deck, but more often on a modern ship it is a steel bunk frame triced up against the side of the casemate in the daytime, lowered at night. Sometimes—but rarely for a boot—it may be a cot, a folding cot like an army cot which can be spread out anywhere space can be found on the deck.

Life aboard a modern man-of-war is certainly no soft bed of down. Men-of-war are built for fighting, not for pleasure; there are no chairs about the decks, not even benches topside, save now and again a circular plank of wood rimming a barbette. The sailor sleeps in his hammock or in his bunk or cot; he lives out of his sea bag, hung in a "bag alley" or wherever space will permit, and from a tiny locker, perhaps 18 inches by 24; and he may eat from a wooden mess table with folding legs, which, when meals are over, can be stowed out of the way triced up against the overhead.

On our most modern fighting ships berthing and messing spaces are separate; some ships even have the cafeteria system. But generally the sailor eats and sleeps and lives in the same compartment which to him may be "home" for all or most of his hitch. "Home" may be a 6-inch gun casemate with steel bulkheads (walls) and overhead (ceiling) and a linoleum-covered steel deck. The big shiny breech of a gun may be his constant companion; certainly his first and last memories of navy life will be of white paint and shining metal and of the glare of naked electric light bulbs (softened after taps to the blue glow of the battle lights); of a compartment as spick-and-span as a new pin.

There is a great premium on neatness and cleanliness in life aboard ship, and the boot will also find that he lives by a rigid routine.

The day starts early aboard a man-of-war; at 4 A.M., or sometimes before, the lights are shining in the galley and the ship's cooks are hard at work getting breakfast ready for scores of men with capacious appetites. Three quarters of an hour later the buglers, the police petty officers of the ship (assistants to the "chief policeman," the master-at-arms) and the boatswain's mates with their pipes have to show a leg, and about 5 A.M. the "saddest bugle call" of all—reveille—echoes through the loud speakers. The "hand" (a seaman is also a "hand") lashes up his hammock or trices up his bunk, gulps a scalding cup of steaming "jamoke" (coffee or "java"), takes a smoke, and turns to. He's at work on

the decks, sweeping them, wetting them down with salt
water from a deck hose, scrubbing them thoroughly,
and then drying them with a squilgee (pronounced
squee-gee) long before the average man is awake.

When the decks are clean and dry the wash-deck gear
is stowed away; the sailors roll down their bell-bottomed
trousers, put on their socks and shoes, and if the day
is fair, take the canvas gun covers and hatch hoods off
the guns and hatches. At seven the late sleepers—those
who have had a night watch, have to turn out, and
from then on the day may go something like this:

DAILY ROUTINE IN PORT		DAILY ROUTINE AT SEA
Breakfast	0730	Breakfast
Colors	0800	Relieve the watch
Turn to; shine brightwork	0815	Turn to; shine brightwork
Sick call	0830	Sick call
Knock off brightwork	0845	Knock off brightwork
Quarters for muster and inspection; setting-up exercises	0915	Quarters for muster and inspection; setting-up exercises
General drills or General quarters (Battle stations)	0940	General drills or General quarters (Battle stations)
	1000	Relieve the wheel and lookout
Retreat from drill or General quarters; mast for punishment	1130	Retreat from drill or General quarters; mast for punishment
Mess gear	1145	Mess gear

DAILY ROUTINE IN PORT		DAILY ROUTINE AT SEA
Dinner	1200	Dinner
Band call	1230	Relieve the watch; band call
Turn to; sweep decks	1300	Turn to; sweep decks
Drill	1315	Drill
	1400	Relieve the wheel and lookout
Retreat from drill	1430	Retreat from drill
Knock off work	1600	Relieve the watch
Lay aft the liberty party	1630	Sweep down; knock off work
Clear up decks	1730	Clear up decks
Mess gear	1745	Mess gear
Supper	1800	Supper; relieve wheel and lookout
Sweep decks; scrub clothes	1830	Sweep decks; scrub clothes
Movies; hammocks	1930	Movies or drill; hammocks
Muster the anchor watch; searchlight drills	2000	Relieve the watch; muster the lifeboat's crew
Taps	2200	Taps

This is a hard schedule, particularly at present, when the Navy's guns are speaking in earnest. But the Navy man is always on the move; not for him the static discipline of an army camp. In port and when possible there are motion pictures, the latest and best, nearly every night; there are "Happy Hours" of amateur, and sometimes professional entertainment, boxing, wrestling, etc.; there is "swimming call"; there is liberty ashore in familiar or foreign ports. The schedule is strenuous, particularly nowadays, when the training year is one long round of many hours at general quarters (battle stations), of "Condition one" (standing by the guns), of maneuvers, of day and night drills—all aiming towards that goal of battle efficiency. But it is a schedule which brings its own reward in the increased knowledge of the job, in intervals of delightful relaxation, in hard exercise and hard work and big appetites, and finally in the climactic thundering drama of battle practice when the racing screws pound the ocean into foam, when the great guns speak towards the far horizons.

The average youngster finds all sorts of unexpected complexities in a seagoing life. He learns to wash in a bucket (though most ships in the Navy now have a limited number of showers and washbasins); he discovers that the toilets aboard ship are known as "heads" (because, in the old sailing-ship days, they used to be located in the extreme head or forepart of a ship). He learns to scrub his own clothes; all large ships and most small ones now have ship's laundries but he finds that a good scrub brush, a cake of salt-water soap, and some "elbow-grease," plus the bright sunshine of a clear day can get his whites whiter than any mechanical contrivance can possibly do. He discovers that the ship usually has a little ship's paper, published periodically, and a daily digest of world news received via radio and printed on the ship's printing press or mimeographed.

He can buy ice cream or soda water practically at cost at the canteen, nearly anything he wants at the ship's store (including cigarettes, tax-free at 5 to 8 cents a package). He can get reading matter at the library and can take his personal problems to the ship's chaplain who regularly holds Sunday services on all larger ships, or to his division officer.

The complement of a ship is normally divided into departments—gunnery, navigation, engineer, construction and repair, supply, medical, etc.—and subdivided into divisions.

When the young sailor is assigned to a working division he may find himself in any one of a variety of occupations. A division is a unit of the ship's company which may number from 20 to more than 100 men; it is numbered or lettered according to the part of the ship it works in or keeps clean; it has its own officers and its own particular cleaning, drill and battle stations, and each man in it has a specific job.

There are deck divisions and there are engineering divisions—"deck gang" and "black gang"—and the boot who enters the one or the other immediately finds himself classified, like the sheep from the goats. If he stays in the "black gang" he wears a single thin red stripe around his left shoulder where the sleeve joins the shoulder; if he stays in the deck forces the stripe is white and is around the right shoulder.

If he reports to a big ship, and whenever possible boots are sent first to the "battlewagons" (battleships), the youngster may find himself in the "1st Division," the "2nd Division," etc.; and he will discover that the

"1st Division" takes care of the forward part of the ship; it scrubs the forecastle; shines the brasswork forward; stands by the ground tackle (anchor gear) when the ship is coming into port or leaving port, and mans No. 1 Turret in practice or in action. The "2nd Division" mans No. 2 Turret and keeps the ship clean around it, etc., until away in the stern of the ship, perhaps the 4th or 5th Division may work. Below decks he will find that the Boiler Division is called the "B Division"; the electricians are grouped in the "E Division," etc. There are many specialized divisions, such as the "F Division" (Fire Control Division), composed of many of the ship's elite, the rangefinder operators who measure, with the help of the ship's rangefinders, the distance in yards to another ship or a target, and the other highly skilled and highly trained specialists who assist in controlling the fire of the ship's guns. The marines aboard battleships and cruisers form a special division of their own, which mans some of the broadside or anti-aircraft guns.

Each division is in turn divided into watches and sections. There are usually two sections to the port watch, two to the starboard watch. The terms port and starboard watch no longer retain the same meaning they had in the old sailing-ship days; they are simply a convenient carry-over from the past and are now a method of designating portions of the ship's crews. The sailor is assigned "liberty" or shore leave by sections; usually two out of four of the ship's sections, or one watch, or about one-half the crew are allowed ashore at any one time; occasionally three out of four sections are given simultaneous liberty. This may be during daylight hours until a certain specified time (6 P.M. or 1800; 10 P.M. or 2200; midnight or 2400), or overnight. The sections that remain aboard are known as "duty sections," others are "liberty sections." The sailor is also entitled to thirty days' leave or vacation every year when naval operations and duties permit. The bluejacket, when on liberty or shore leave, usually carries a small liberty card, colored, according to the section in which the sailor is assigned, which he must be prepared to show to the officer of the deck when he goes ashore and to drop in a special box when he returns aboard.

Each bluejacket, in addition to his battle station (known in our Navy as "General quarters"), has a specific station for other emergencies or drills. He must go to such and such a place, handle a fire hose, a fire extinguisher, or an ax, etc., in case of fire; in case of collision he may be assigned to handle a part of the collision mat—a great canvas, rope-thrummed mat which, by means of ropes and handling gear, can be hauled into place over the hole in the ship's side to stop the inrush of water. These and other drills are practiced at least once a week, sometimes more often; there is a premium upon speed and efficiency which pays dividends in the case of a real emergency. In addition each bluejacket has a certain specific watch station; in port he may be a messenger, a signalman, or a member of the anchor watch (which doesn't watch the anchor, as the name might imply to the landsman, but is simply a small group of men mustered each evening to be on hand in case of need). At sea the bluejacket

may stand watch as fireman in the boiler room for four
hours; he may stand a trick as lookout at the masthead
or in the bridge wings for two hours; or he may steer
the ship. His tours of duty are known as "watches";
normally his tour of duty or watch at sea is four hours
on and twelve off, day and night, but this may be
altered.

The sailor must mind his *P's* and *Q's*. He must obey
quickly and cheerfully, with an "Aye aye, sir"—meaning "the order is understood and will be carried out."
He must remember, when aboard ship, to salute an
officer the first time he sees him during the day, to
salute the captain at all times, to salute the officer of the
deck and the colors (two separate salutes) when leaving
or coming aboard the ship, to stand at attention when
an officer enters a compartment or when addressed by
an officer.

There are many customs aboard ship; the discipline,
far less formal, particularly aboard small ships, than
that in most land armies, though no less real, is one
which requires instinctive and absolute but intelligent
obedience. It is a discipline that is concerned with results; the sailor must know his job, for every man aboard
ship is a cog in a machine; his ship's fate and his shipmates' lives may depend upon his efficiency.

There are many "don'ts" and some penalties. Drinking and liquor are taboo. Cursing and gambling and
slovenliness are sins. Desertion is unpardonable;
A.W.O.L. or A.O.L. (Absent without leave, or Absent
over leave) are the causes of more courts-martial than
probably any other offense, and women, it has been

found, rarely teach the young boot the way to promotion and pay. The "Articles for the Government of the Navy" upon which the sacrosanct Navy Regulations are based are a category of "don'ts," and there are no less than twenty-two different offenses for which a general court-martial may impose the death penalty, with mutiny heading the list and murder ending it. Such severe penalties are rarely imposed, however, even in war, and they rarely need to be. There are, however, less severe penalties for offenders, including prison terms in naval prisons.

The process of discipline in the Navy is usually rather sure and swift, and generally surprisingly fair. Sea lawyers have less chance to circumvent justice by legalistic devices; the turn of a pretty ankle or the lift of a skirt cannot distract a jury's attention, for there is no jury, and relatively rarely are women called as witnesses.

Punishments or dispositions of cases awaiting judgment are decided by the captain of a vessel or station at a session called "mast" (also a carry-over from the old sailing-ship days) held once a day or when necessary. The commanding officer has himself considerable power; indeed, aboard ship he is supreme. He can reduce any rating established by himself; confine a prisoner to the brig not exceeding ten days; give him "B. and W."—solitary confinement on bread and water for no more than five days; deprive the offender of shore liberty, or require the performance of extra duty. Or, if the offense is severe enough, a deck, summary, or general court-martial can be ordered which can impose punishments varying from forfeiture of pay, to discharge from the service, imprisonment or death, sentences which, however, are subject to approval or commutation by higher authority.

Discharges are of numerous classes, some of them of a disciplinary nature and carrying a stigma which will be a handicap in civilian life. They are classified from "Honorable," "Good," "Indifferent," through various special order and undesirable discharges, to "Dishonorable" or "Bad Conduct" discharges which can be awarded only by courts-martial. During the 1941 fiscal year there were only sixty-nine dishonorable discharges, 1,420 bad conduct discharges, 379 undesirable discharges, 20,157 honorable discharges. The percentage of disciplinary discharges to total discharges was small.

The apprentice seaman who joins his ship with the single thin white stripe around his cuff automatically becomes, after four months, a seaman second class or a fireman third class, and in addition to that red or white stripe around his shoulder which indicates whether he belongs to the "black gang" or the "deck gang" he adds another thin white stripe to his cuff. When he is again promoted to a first-class seaman or a first-class nonrated man in other branches he adds a third thin white stripe to his cuff.

The sailor's uniform tells a great deal to those who know it. All bluejackets wear the same standard uniforms—navy-blue jumper with V neck and middy collar, with the three white stripes of tape around the collar and a white star in either corner; blue bell-bottomed trousers; black neckerchief tied in a flat square knot

around the collar; black shoes and socks; blue flat hat
with a cap ribbon. In summer or warm weather the uniform is white with blue markings and designations, but

CHIEF COMMISSARY
STEWARD

ELECTRICIAN'S
MATE
1ST CLASS

PHARMACIST'S
MATE
2ND CLASS

PRINTER
3RD CLASS

OFFICER'S
STEWARD
3RD CLASS

4 YEARS'
SERVICE

8 YEARS'
SERVICE

12 YEARS'
SERVICE

Navy Rating Badges and Service Stripes

of the same general cut. In very cold weather sailors
wear a peacoat or short mackinaw with black navy buttons; they have no overcoats. Aboard ships undress uniforms, of rougher material and without the collar markings of the dress uniforms, are usually worn.

All enlisted men of both the Navy and the Coast
Guard except chief petty officers wear this same type

of uniform. The chief petty officer—the Navy's equivalent of a "top sergeant" or master sergeant wears a uniform that is in cut somewhat similar to the officer's. The
trousers are blue slacks without cuffs; the jacket is a
double-breasted blue jacket with brass buttons; the cap
is visored without the gold braid of the officer's cap,
but with a gold anchor insignia pinned upon the front.

A chief petty officer is the highest rating to which an
enlisted man can rise; directly above chief petty officers in the hierarchy of rank of the Navy are warrant
officers and officers.

Below chief petty officers are petty officers, first class;
petty officers, second class; petty officers, third class (all
roughly corresponding to sergeants and corporals in
the Army); and the nonrated men who are also divided
into first, second, and third class. Except for the chief
petty officers, whose uniform as just described, is distinctive, the uniforms of the petty officers are identical
with those of the nonrated men, and their ratings can
be distinguished only by the insignia on their sleeves.

But the sleeve insignia and cap ribbons tell a great
deal. The cap ribbon, worn only with the blue flat hat,
indicates a sailor's ship or station; the gold lettering
on the black band may read *U.S.S. Mississippi, or U. S.
Naval Training Station*. (In these times of war and
emergency cap ribbons are not always a faithful
index of a sailor's station; to prevent foreign spies
from identifying men-of-war in port cap ribbons may
simply bear the designation *U. S. Navy*.) The stripes
around the shoulder (worn by the nonrated man only)

indicate whether the bluejacket is in the deck force or the engineering force. The thin cuff stripes indicate whether he is a first, second, or third-class nonrated man. If the bluejacket has a long, red diagonal stripe on the left sleeve of his blue uniform (a similar blue stripe on a white uniform) he has served a "hitch," or four years. Another stripe is added for each four years; by counting them you can see approximately how many years the wearer has served in the Navy. If the stripes are of gold you are looking at someone who has, indeed, a top-notch record, for to wear those coveted gold "hash marks" the wearer must have:

Served continuously in the Navy for at least twelve years
Won the maximum number of three good-conduct awards, one for each enlistment
A perfect record for sobriety
A perfect record for obedience
A proficiency record of not less than 3.5 on basis of 4.0 as perfect.

The very large number of gold "hash marks" that you will see when the fleet's in is sufficient indication that the Navy's chief petty officers and first-class petty officers are of very high type.

The sleeve designations of petty officers—chevrons and insignia—are worn on the right sleeves of petty officers in the seaman branch, on the left sleeves of all others. There are six main branches, each with various specialty ratings: the seaman branch; the artificer branch; the artificer branch—Engineer force; the spe-

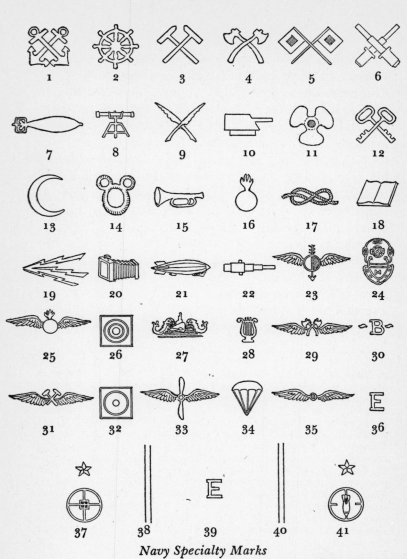

Navy Specialty Marks

[See caption on opposite page.]

cial branch; the commissary branch; and the aviation branch. In addition there is the messman branch (for Filipinos and Negroes). The young apprentice seaman picks out one or the other of these branches and commences to fit himself for the climb up the ladder of promotion. As he goes up he advances from pay grade to pay grade and his rating badge changes to show his rating. The specialty mark in that rating badge, such as a symbol of a bugle for a bugler, remains the same, however, unless the sailor should change his specialty. The specialty marks illustrated on page 52 graphically portray the type of the bluejacket's job. The number of chevrons beneath the specialty mark indicate whether the bluejacket is a first, second, or third-class petty officer. One chevron is for a third-class, two for a second, three for a first. An eagle, or "the bird," as the sailors call it, tops the whole, and a chief petty officer

---

1. Boatswain's Mate, Coxwain—2. Quarter Master—3. Shipfitter, Molder, Metalsmith—4. Painter, Patternmaker, Carpenter's Mate—5. Signalman—6. Gunner's Mate—7. Torpedoman—8. Fire Controlman—9. Yeoman—10. Turret Captain—11. Machinist's Mate, Boilermaker, Watertender—12. Storekeeper—13. Ship's Cook, Baker—14. Sailmaker's Mate—15. Buglemaster, Bugler—16. Seaman Gunner—17. Ex-apprentice—18. Printer—19. Radioman—20. Photographer—21. Rigid Airship—22. Gun Captain—23. Aerographer—24. Master Diver—25. Ordnance Man, Aviation—26. Expert Rifleman—27. Submarine—28. Bandmaster, Musician—29. Carpenter's Mate, Aviation—30. Bomber, Mechanic—31. Metalsmith, Aviation—32. Sharpshooter—33. Machinist's Mate, Aviation—34. Parachute Man—35. General Utility, Aviation—36. Navy Excellence, Efficiency, Gunnery (white)—37. Gunpointer, 1st class—38. Shoulder Braid (red) Engineering Branch—39. Navy Excellence, Efficiency, Engineering (red)—40. Shoulder Braid (white) Seaman Branch—41. Master Horizontal Bomber.

SERGEANT
MAJOR

FIRST
SERGEANT

PLATOON
SERGEANT

SERGEANT

CORPORAL

2ND LEADER
MARINE BAND

MUSICIAN
MARINE BAND

MILITARY
POLICE

SERVICE STRIPE
ONE FOR EACH
FOUR YEARS

MASTER
TECHNICAL
SERGEANT

TECHNICAL
SERGEANT

STAFF
SERGEANT

PRIVATE
FIRST CLASS

Marine Corps Ratings

has a white arch above his chevrons and beneath his "bird" which gives him further distinction.

Seamen also wear on their sleeves various distinguishing marks, such as "E" for excellence in gunnery or engineering. These are awarded for proficiency in certain subjects.

The marine's uniform, of course, differs from the navy man's. The campaign, or field uniform is khaki, like the Army's, though with marine buttons and insignia; the dress uniform is the famous dark-blue blouse (known as "serge blue") with the yellow and red sleeve markings and chevrons, the light-blue trousers (known as "field blue"), the white cloth belt with highly polished buckle, the black shoes, and the visored cap. Marine ratings, pay, and promotion system are much the same as the Army's; the recruit enlists as a private at $21 a month (for four months) and then starts up the ladder of promotion and pay in any one of seven different branches he may select: the musician branch; the signal and radio branch; quartermaster branch; line branch; paymaster branch; aviation branch; or mess branch. The Corps is small but it is versatile; these "soldiers of the sea" utilize both army and navy schools and also some specialist schools of their own.

The sleeve markings are distinctive and more simple than those of the bluejacket. A single yellow chevron (worn on both sleeves) indicates a private first class (or equivalent in other branches, *viz.*, assistant cook; field music, first class); two chevrons are a corporal; three, a sergeant; three with a semicircular arch or straight bar connecting the ends of the lowest one, a staff sergeant;

three chevrons, the semicircular arch device and one chevron beneath it, a first sergeant or its equivalent; the same, with two chevrons beneath the arch, a master sergeant or sergeant major.

Pay, in both the Navy and Marine Corps, depends in part upon rating, in part upon length of service; all enlisted men are divided into pay grades in which all ratings and nonratings of all branches are included.

RATES OF PAY

Pay Grade	Base Pay Per Month	Class or Rating
1	$126	Chief Petty Officers (permanent appointment), Sergeant Majors or equivalent in Marines
1–A	$99	Chief Petty Officers (Acting Appointments)
2	$84	Petty officers, first class; officers' stewards and cooks, first class; musicians, first class; First Sergeants or equivalent in Marines
3	$72	Petty officers, second class; officers' cooks and stewards, second class; musicians, first class; staff sergeants or equivalent in Marines
4	$60	Petty officers, third class; firemen, first class; officers' stewards and cooks, third class

Pay Grade	Base Pay Per Month	Class or Rating
5 (4 for Marines)	$54	Nonrated men, first class (except firemen, first class, and musicians, first class); firemen, second class; musicians, second class; mess attendants, first class; sergeants or equivalent in Marines
5 (For Marines only)	$42	Corporals or equivalent in Marines
6	$36	Nonrated men, second class (except firemen, second class, and musicians, second class); firemen, third class; mess attendants, second class
6 (For Marines only)	$30	Privates, first class or equivalent
7	$21	Nonrated men, third class (except firemen, third class); mess attendants, third class; privates in Marines

In addition to the base pay per month listed above, there are certain allowances or additions to the pay of every enlisted man. Dental and medical care is free; the first outfit of the navy recruit is free; the marine gets a certain clothing allowance every year; enlisted men receive rations of food free; sometimes they receive cash, fifty cents a day, instead of rations; sometimes when an enlisted man is on certain types of duty ashore he may receive from $1.95 to $3.75 a day for subsistence and quarters. There are extra allowances, varying from $2 a month for each medal of honor, etc., to $30 for divers (plus $5 an hour for all dives beyond depths of 90 feet); there is extra pay for submarine duty and flying duty and many other allowances. The enlisted man also receives longevity pay in addition to base pay and allowances; that is, he gets 10 per cent increase after four years' service and 5 per cent for each four years thereafter up to a maximum of 25 per cent. (This means, for instance, $157.50 a month for a chief petty officer with sixteen years' service, plus allowances.) If he re-enlists within three months of the date of expiration of his previous enlistment he receives a re-enlistment bonus.

Upon completion of twenty years' service, an enlisted man, "if physically and otherwise qualified to perform duty in time of war, may transfer to the Fleet Reserve and receive one-half his base pay." After thirty years' service, "an enlisted man may retire on three-fourths of the pay of his rating, including all permanent additions, plus $15.75 allowance in lieu of quarters, fuel, and light, making a retirement pay of $133.88 a month if the retiring man is a chief petty officer with a permanent appointment."

There is no extra allowance for married sailors or marines; indeed the Navy strongly discourages nonrated men and lower-class petty officers from marrying, since the sailor's pay—though it is the highest naval pay in the world—will not adequately support a wife and family. Nevertheless some 17 per cent of the Navy's enlisted men are married, and the married ones make good

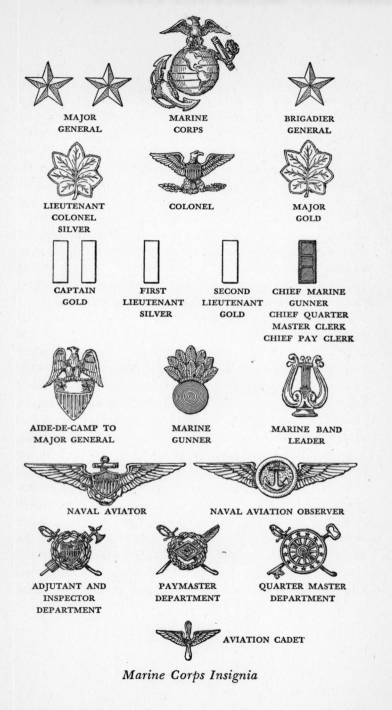

MAJOR
GENERAL

MARINE
CORPS

BRIGADIER
GENERAL

LIEUTENANT
COLONEL
SILVER

COLONEL

MAJOR
GOLD

CAPTAIN
GOLD

FIRST
LIEUTENANT
SILVER

SECOND
LIEUTENANT
GOLD

CHIEF MARINE
GUNNER
CHIEF QUARTER
MASTER CLERK
CHIEF PAY CLERK

AIDE-DE-CAMP TO
MAJOR GENERAL

MARINE
GUNNER

MARINE BAND
LEADER

NAVAL AVIATOR

NAVAL AVIATION OBSERVER

ADJUTANT AND
INSPECTOR
DEPARTMENT

PAYMASTER
DEPARTMENT

QUARTER MASTER
DEPARTMENT

AVIATION CADET

Marine Corps Insignia

dependable petty officers, though they are inclined to be somewhat restless if their ships are away from home ports for very protracted periods.

A sailor specializes in the branch of service which he wishes to follow by study in navy schools, by practical experience aboard ship, by correspondence courses conducted by the Navy, by study in his spare time. He must pass written examinations and give practical demonstration of his qualification for advancement, and must serve a certain length of time in each rating, and he may have, at times, to wait for vacancies in the rating above him before he can be promoted. But unlike the Army, once the sailor has gotten his rating he keeps it regardless of the ship or station upon which he may be assigned to serve; he can be broken in rating not by reason of change of station but only for disciplinary reasons.

There are many, many service schools in the Navy and some fifty-five different trades are taught, from cooking and baking to machine-shop work. Some few recruits are sent directly from the training stations to service schools which give primary instruction in certain specialties, but usually a sailor must have experience afloat before he is sent to a special school. Courses vary in length from three weeks to one year (the latter a course for training enlisted aviation pilots at Pensacola), and vary in difficulty from elementary grammar and arithmetic to practical electrical and mechanical engineering.

Service schools are divided into three general classifications: Class A schools for elementary instruction in certain specialties to recruits; Class B schools to supplement the training afloat by giving more advanced instruction in certain specialties to selected, experienced enlisted men; and Class C schools to give advanced instruction in certain technical specialties which are not normally a part of shipboard instruction. The schools are divided as follows:

CLASS A

Group I Electrical
         Ordnance
Group II Communication
         Clerical

Group III Machinists
         Metalworkers
         Woodworkers
         Buglers
         Hospital Corpsmen
         Musicians

CLASS B

Cooks and Bakers
Electrical Interior Communications
Fire Control
Gyro compass
Officers' Cooks and Stewards

Optical
Sound Motion-picture Technicians
Stenography
Torpedomen

CLASS C

Aerographers
Airship Training
Aviation Pilot Training
Aviation Instrument
Aviation Mechanics
Aviation Ordnance
Buglemasters

Deep-sea Divers
Dental Technicians
Naval Academy Preparatory
Optical
Parachute Material
Pharmicist's Mates

CLASS C

Photographers   Recruiters
Slide Film   Submarine Training
Radio Material

Applicants for these schools must have good records, must pass classification tests, have the equivalent of at least a grammar school education, and have aptitude for the particular specialty which he wishes to study. The schools are located all over the country, with most of them at Norfolk, San Diego, or Pensacola.

The enlisted man can, therefore, make his way up the service ladder with every help from the government. He can enlist in the Navy, learn a trade, and still end his six years of service young enough to practice that trade in civilian life; or he can enlist and re-enlist and make the Navy a career. He must, of course, learn his *military* duties and know them thoroughly, but his advancement depends, not only on knowing them, but also on knowing his *specialist* duties. If he is intelligent, ambitious, hard-working, and obedient; if he has character and cheerfulness, he may be able to advance from a boot to a first-class petty officer—from $21 a month to $84—in his first enlistment.

The privileges and prerogatives of a chief petty officer, with his separate mess and living quarters, are then before him; he may, too, become a warrant officer if he works hard and can pass a professional examination, and even promotion to officer rank is not beyond him. Or if he shows particular aptitude and intelligence while he is still a young boot (under 20 years) and can pass a preliminary test he may apply for instruction at the enlisted men's Naval Academy preparatory school. One hundred enlisted men of the Navy and Marine Corps are eligible yearly for appointment to Annapolis, and the Navy takes pains to instruct its most likely candidates, those who have had nine months' sea duty as enlisted men and are of officer caliber. After their schooling these applicants must take the regular Naval Academy entrance examinations; if they pass, they doff their sailor's blues and become Midshipmen, U.S.N. They are on the way to promotion and pay, and the world is their oyster.

CHAPTER THREE

THE OFFICER

IT IS by no means enough that an officer of the Navy should be a capable mariner. He must be that, of course, but also a great deal more. He should be as well a gentleman of liberal education, refined manners, punctilious courtesy, and the nicest sense of personal honor."

John Paul Jones' qualifications for the naval officer, as listed by Augustus C. Buell, are as cogent and valid today as when they were first expressed in those years when the canny Scot was writing history with his imperishable spirit and the guns of the old *Bon Homme Richard.*

Today, a "capable mariner" is only the first of many requirements, and perhaps not the most important. It is no longer enough to be master of the wind and tide, to be able to impale the shining glory of a star upon the mathematics of navigation. The modern naval officer must be a technician; indeed his capabilities as a technician must, perhaps, transcend his capabilities as a seaman. The modern naval officer must be more than a naval officer; he must understand the new-found imperial power of the plane; he must comprehend the slow but immutable workings of economic and political forces; his kingdom is as broad as the mind of man.

Gone are the days when tactics were compressed into

the phrase that no commander could go far wrong if he laid his ship alongside an enemy's. Gone are the days when a smoking pistol and a bloody cutlass and a ready leg over the enemy's bulwark meant leadership. Gone are the days when discipline was "fifty with the cat," and an officer's education was gained with the stimulating help of a rope's end.

A naval officer today is a Jack-of-all-trades, but not, as that phrase implies, master of none. If he is good he must be master of many. One thing he must have in common with the old sea dogs of the past; he must have courage and character, courage, moral as well as physical, character, rugged in strength and endurance and patience, undeviating in loyalty.

The naval officer today must fit himself to handle men and ships and fleets. But this implies a variety of duties. Ashore he may be called upon to serve in any capacity from inspector of a steel plant manufacturing navy matériel to Chief of Naval Operations, a position that entails, primarily, knowledge of the legislative processes of democracy, knowledge of government and politics, knowledge of economics and labor. Afloat he may be called upon to navigate a division of S-boats (submarines) to Manila, a job that requires knowledge of the eternal verities of geography, of astronomy, of mathematics, of wind and weather and tide. He may become radio officer of a battleship and experiment in the strange and half-explored world of space. He may be pilot of a fighting plane, hurled into space from a catapult, leaping above the sea from a carrier deck, winging wide and far above the crests of ocean. Or he may handle the frightening, caged forces imprisoned within the engineering plant of a modern ship. And entrusted to his care, a creature of his destiny, is perhaps a $100,-000,000 battleship, product of all arts and sciences, and her crew of 1,500 men, sons of the nation, cross section of America. The fleet is his—and the modern fleet, with its ships and men and planes, is indeed so much a symbol of a nation's power, so great a trump in the unending game of power politics that of the contemporary naval commander it can be truly said, as it was said of Jellicoe at Jutland, that he is "the only man who can lose a war in an afternoon."

Such responsibilities require a Spartan and inclusive thoroughness of preparation. The candidates for power and responsibility and possible greatness must be schooled in the meaning of such terms; greatness is rarely thrust upon a child still wet behind the ears and raw with ignorance.

A naval officer's education is a slow, long, and painful task which is never completed.

There are several routes to a commission; to a commission in the Naval Reserve these roads are various and relatively easy; to a commission in the Regular Navy they are but two and they are hard.

Annapolis, long called the cradle of the service, is indeed, the chief source of all American naval officers. Unlike our Army which has a large proportion of non-West Pointers in its officer ranks, unlike the Marine Corps where many officers rise from the ranks, the Regular Navy of the United States is officered very largely by graduates of the United States Naval Academy. Naval

Academy graduates control the Navy, run the Navy; without them there could be no Navy.

For the fiscal year 1940, the annual report of Rear Admiral Chester W. Nimitz, Chief of the Bureau of Navigation (which handles the Navy's personnel), makes this abundantly clear.

"With the exception of the medical, dental, and chaplain corps, the Naval Academy continues to be the basic source of supply for officers of the line and staff corps," the report states. "The training, indoctrination, esprit de corps, love of the service, attributes of leadership and appreciation of responsibilities to the Navy and to the nation, inculcated at the Naval Academy, insure a high standard and superior military character in the graduates; and assure a source of supply of young officers second to none.

"All officers commissioned in the line of the Navy during the fiscal year were, accordingly, graduates of the Naval Academy. In the staff corps, five naval constructors, one civil engineer, and twenty-seven supply officers were commissioned by transfer of officers from the line.

". . . of a total of sixty-six appointments to the supply corps twenty-seven were by transfer from the line and thirty-nine were by appointment from graduates of Naval R.O.T.C. units after careful selection from the list of applicants. There was one appointment to the civil engineer corps by transfer from the line.

"In addition there were sixty-nine medical officers, twenty-nine dental officers, and seven chaplains commissioned from civil life."

Entry into the Naval Academy is directly from civilian life, from the enlisted men of the Navy and Marine Corps, from the enlisted men of the Naval Reserve and the Marine Corps Reserve, and from among the honor graduates of educational institutions and members of the Naval Reserve Officers' Training Corps.

All these candidates must meet the same requirements. All must be between 17 and 21 years of age at entrance. They must qualify mentally for admission under regulations defined by the Navy, which change from time to time, but which require either examination, presentation of a school certificate and passing a substantiating examination, or presentation of a certificate alone.

The methods of qualifying mentally depend in large part upon the character and quality of the applicant's previous education. If the school he has attended is on the list of so-called "accredited schools" and its standards are known to be exceptionally high, and if the applicant's marks at that school have been exceptionally high he may be admitted by certificate only, but more generally examinations are given. These examinations, whose scope and character are covered in a formidable little pamphlet, entitled, *Regulations Governing the Admission of Candidates into the United States Naval Academy as Midshipmen and Sample Examination Papers* (which can be procured from the Bureau of Navigation, Navy Department, Washington, D. C., without cost), are difficult and extensive. Many candidates fail them.

Others cannot meet the other requirements. The applicant must be unmarried, must never have been married, and must agree not to marry within two years after his graduation from the Naval Academy. He must be a citizen, of good character, and he must present references who can attest to his character.

He must, if he meets all other requirements, take a strenuous physical examination at Annapolis. The eye tests are particularly thorough and exacting. The candidate can take a preliminary physical examination in or near his home community to determine whether or not he has any obvious physical defects which would cause his later rejection at Annapolis, but this preliminary examination is in no sense final.

Entrance to Annapolis is made by a system of appointments, many of them political in character. Every Senator, Representative, Delegate in Congress, and the Vice-President are allowed under the law a total of six appointments actually in the Naval Academy at any one time. The President has a District of Columbia and at-large appointive power (four for the former; twenty-five for the latter). In addition, 100 enlisted men of the Navy and Marine Corps who are selected as a result of competitive examinations and who can meet all the other requirements, can be appointed each year. One hundred others, also selected as a result of competitive examinations, may be appointed from the enlisted men of the Naval and Marine Corps Reserves, and twenty appointments can go to honor graduates of civilian educational institutions and members of the Naval R.O.T.C. One native Puerto Rican; four residents of Puerto Rico, not native; and four Filipinos may be at the Academy simultaneously.

Senators' and Congressmen's appointees, because the competition is frequently great, are often selected as a result of competitive examinations, and these competitive examinations given under the jurisdiction of the Senator or Congressman concerned, are the regular Naval Academy entrance examinations, and hence the winning candidate is not required to take those examinations again.

The system of appointments is somewhat confusing, and those exercising the appointive powers have often done so in various ways. With the years, however, and with a rigid insistence upon standard entrance requirements, the type of human material secured by the Academy has increased in caliber, and qualifications have become more standardized than in the past.

The law now provides for a total of 3,702 midshipmen at the Naval Academy at any one time, but actually there are never that many there, and in October, 1941, there were 3,100.

The course of instruction is four years (three during the emergency); the successful candidate, when he comes to Annapolis for his physical examination, must, if he passes, be prepared to stay; he must sign articles promising to serve in the Navy at the pleasure of the President, and he must make a cash deposit of $100 to help to pay for his initial "outfit." (An additional $250 is credited to the entering midshipman by the government and is later deducted from his pay in monthly installments.)

The successful candidates are sworn in usually in

June and July, and become Midshipmen, Fourth Class, United States Navy. They are probably the only college students in the country, except for students at West Point and the Coast Guard Academy, who draw pay while studying. Yet they earn that pay of $780 a year, and they are not, in any real sense of the word, college students, although graduates of the Naval Academy, past, present, and future, are now entitled to put the letters "B.S." (Bachelor of Science) after their names.

The Fourth Classman at Annapolis is also known as a "plebe"; he rates lower in the scale of rank than anything in the world, except possibly a marine, as he discovers to his sorrow! When the youth finishes that grueling first year at the Academy he becomes a Third Classman, or youngster; after two years he becomes a Second Classman; and in his fourth and final year of study he is that high and exalted personage—a First Classman. The normal course of four years, with one class being graduated every June, has been shortened during the present emergency, and the Class of 1941 was graduated in February, four months early.

The student at Annapolis learns military duties and professional duties. As a plebe he is hazed, officially and unofficially; he must stand up when upper classmen come in his room; he must say "Sir" to everybody but the ship's cat; he must learn "who is the king of Siam" (the answer—"I am, by God, I am"); he must learn naval terminology and live in the great barracks of Bancroft Hall as if he were aboard a ship, calling floors "decks," telling time by "bells," and absorbing the customs and the traditions of the service.

The plebe has his choice of four languages for study: French, Spanish, German, or Italian, and he is assigned to companies and battalions by the language he chooses. The midshipmen are organized on a regimental basis in four battalions and twelve companies; they march to and from all recitations. Most of the plebe's initial drill is, ironically enough, on land. Later he takes to the boats, pulling boats and sailboats in the waters of the Severn. He makes his first deep-sea cruise at the end of his first year of study—a three months' trip on battleships of training units of the fleet. After more than a year in uniform he gets his first extended leave of about thirty days (also likely to be curtailed during this period of emergency).

At the end of youngster year, during his third summer in the Navy, the midshipman takes a coastal cruise aboard a destroyer—his first deep-sea introduction to small vessels—gets his first flight instruction, actually spending about ten hours in the air in naval patrol planes as observer, bomber, and navigator (but not as pilot), and helps to indoctrinate, organize, and train the new incoming plebe class.

At the end of their second-class year, the summer is spent in another three-month deep-sea cruise aboard battle-wagons in which the midshipmen, soon to become officers, actually take the stations, and learn the duties of officers aboard ship.

Thus academic and classroom study is interspersed with practical work. The course is, however, hard: physically, mentally, and morally the student must progressively pass more and more difficult physical and mental tests. A great deal of ground is covered in many subjects in a short time.

The courses in English and History are elementary, but the professional subjects of seamanship, navigation, gunnery, many kinds of engineering and mathematics, languages, international law, and many other professional subjects are "tough." The course in navigation has recently been much improved and extended so that Annapolis is now thought to be, as it should be, the best navigation school in the world.

After four years of "boning," of customs and vocabulary that are peculiar to Annapolis, the midshipman is glad to exchange his insignia for that of an officer. The actual blue uniforms of the midshipman are almost exactly like those of an officer, but there are many special officers' uniforms and items of equipment which the midshipman does not possess. When his mother and "O.A.O." pin on his shoulder straps by the Japanese Bell (traditionally rung only after a victory over Army) he has passed from the status of fledgling and novitiate to that of a commissioned officer, an Ensign in the United States Navy, in whom the President of the United States, "with the advice and consent of the Senate" (so the Commission reads), reposes "special Trust and Confidence."

Annapolis is almost the sole source of naval officers, but there are a few who rise to the gold braid of rank in the Regular Navy who never attend Annapolis. These few—and there are not many—rise from the ranks, and are known in slang parlance as "mustangs." Some of them are the best deck and division officers and practical engineers the Navy has, but few of them ever become admirals. Theirs is a hard road: from apprentice seaman up the long ladder of nonrated and rated enlisted grades to chief petty officer; then by examination and appointment to warrant officer; finally, if they are under 35, have served not less than four years as warrant officers, and can pass the necessary examinations, to commissions as ensigns.

There are not many who have the qualifications and intelligence to make this really considerable jump from forecastle to wardroom, but some who have do not choose to make it. For it is an idiosyncrasy of the Navy's pay scales that a warrant officer with some years' service usually loses money by becoming an ensign, particularly so since he may be expected in his higher rank to spend more money for social expenses than he would otherwise have had to do. He knows, too, that there is a slight and tacit, but definite gulf between the Naval Academy graduate and the non-graduate; that it is difficult, if not impossible, for the non-graduate to rise to high commissioned rank, and that he may find social discrimination.

Entry into the Navy's commissioned ranks from the Naval Reserve is considerably easier. The Navy's reserves, most of whom because of the present emergency have now been ordered into the active service, are divided into many classifications. Officers of the Reserve are either specialists, such as doctors, dentists, etc., or composed of former navy men, officers who served in the World War, Naval Academy graduates who resigned to enter civilian occupations, graduates of Naval R.O.T.C. schools, Merchant Marine officers, etc. Many of these go to temporary active duty with the Regular Navy at frequent intervals, but few become permanent regular naval officers. Many colleges—among them Yale, Harvard, Northwestern, Georgia School of Technology, University of California, University of Washington, University of California at Los Angeles, Tulane, University of Minnesota, University of Michigan, and University of Oklahoma—now maintain Naval R.O.T.C. courses with a total authorized enrollment of 7,200 students. There were only 5,217 actually enrolled in 1941. Each student devotes approximately four hours per week to naval work during his four-year college course and goes on one or more summer practice cruises. Most of the graduates receive commissions as ensigns in the Naval Reserve; a few are given commissions as ensigns in the Supply Corps of the Regular Navy.

Two other sources of Reserve officers may also contribute slightly to the commissioned personnel of the Regular Navy. One is the newly-established "quickie" course for Reserve ensigns, set up to provide a supply of junior officers during the present emergency. These officers roughly correspond in training and background to the so-called "Ninety-day Wonders" of World War days—young men who were trained in the rudiments of an officer's job in ninety days. The present course of study is also ninety days, but it is preceded by one month's cruise aboard ship which is really the "bait" and "come-on" to attract young men to apply. The cruise serves a useful purpose, however, in that it does give the youngster some practical experience afloat and eliminates the unfit. Upon satisfactory completion of the cruise the applicants are designated as Midshipmen, U. S. Naval Reserve, and are given three months' instruction aboard the training and station ship *Prairie State* in New York; at Northwestern University, Evanston; or at the Naval Academy. Upon satisfactory completion, they are commissioned ensigns in the Reserve.

Aviation cadets—youngsters who can pass the rigid physical requirements and have had two years of college or its equivalent—are another source of Navy officer supply. These youngsters are enlisted in the Naval Reserve for elimination flight training of one month at Naval Reserve aviation fields near their homes; those who pass are sent on to Pensacola for a seven and a half months' intensive training course in flying. They are aviation cadets in the Reserve while at Pensacola; upon successful completion of the course, they are given their wings, commissioned ensigns in the Reserve, and assigned to active duty with the fleet. Upon completion of their tour of active duty they are returned to civilian life, but some who are found suitable are given permanent commissions in the line of the Regular Navy. Some 375 had been so commissioned by January 1, 1941.

It seems very likely that the number of Reserve officers who are thus ordered to active duty and later are given permanent commissions in the Regular Navy will probably increase materially during this present emergency, if the experience of the World War period is a reliable guide.

Still another source of officer material for the Navy is direct appointment, from civilian life, of doctors, dentists, chaplains, and some officers in the supply corps and other specialized corps.

The Marines get twenty-five officers a year from Annapolis, some from private military schools like Virginia Military Institute, a few from the Army, quite a number from the ranks, and some from civilian educational institutions. All of them are given special courses at marine schools.

The life of an officer is a fascinating though a difficult one. When he joins his ship he must turn over his orders to the officer of the deck, the paymaster and the executive officer for notation and endorsement; he must call upon the captain, sword at side, and he should leave cards in the junior officers' mess and wardroom. If he is relatively junior he is assigned by the executive officer to specific duties; if senior, his orders from the Bureau of Navigation in Washington may specifically name him as navigator or engineer officer, etc. He is assigned a stateroom according to his rank and seniority, usually a single room, except on destroyers and submarines and small ships, or in the junior officers' quarters of battleships. If he is a warrant officer he will have a stateroom in the warrant officers' "country" and eat in the warrant officers' mess; if an ensign (aboard a battleship) he will eat in the "J. O." (Junior Officers') mess; usually, if he is a lieutenant, junior grade, or above, he will eat with the executive officer and all other officers, except the captain, in the wardroom. The captain eats alone, in lonely dignity, in his own mess.

The wardroom is the heart of the officers' "country" and the combination living-room-dining-room of most of the officers aboard. The "J. O." mess and the warrant officers' mess fulfill similar functions for the officers of junior rank. Part of each messroom is usually curtained off and is equipped with radio and victrola, easy chairs, magazine racks, bookcases, and card tables where one can nearly always find, in leisure hours, a hand of bridge, or a round of that interminable, indefinable, and omnipresent navy game—"acey-deucey." Mess tables, covered except at mealtime with green baize cloth, occupy the rest of the wardroom.

The wine mess of yesteryear no longer exists aboard naval vessels; since Josephus Daniels made the Navy dry there has been no liquor aboard men-of-war, and the best an officer can do nowadays is Coca-Cola from the special stocks of the wardroom cigar mess.

Each officer pays for his own food, uniforms, and laundry; he "joins" the mess when he joins his ship and pays monthly bills ranging from $15 to $50 for his food. The cigar mess which sells cigarettes, candy, soft drinks, etc., to the officers at cost or slightly more, is an added expense which the officer must pay out of his own pocket. He receives, however, a small subsistence allowance for food.

Life aboard ship is a busy but pleasant one. The officer finds his quarters comfortable if not luxurious. He sleeps on an inner-spring mattress in a ship's bunk which is comfortable and commodious, and which can be fitted with wooden side bars in case it becomes rough. The furniture is metal—metal wardrobe and drawers, a metal desk with a small personal safe, a metal chair, sometimes a leather-cushioned transom beneath the stateroom's porthole. There may be steam or hot-air heating, plus an electric heater. The officer can add to his stateroom such other personal furniture as he desires for which there is room.

Each stateroom usually has a washbasin and running water and there are showers and toilets in the officers' "country."

The work of an officer—a large part of it reports and desk work—requires considerable time, but in normal times there is ample recreation during parties ashore in foreign ports, entertainments aboard, movies nearly every night which the officers, as well as the men, attend, and athletics ashore or on board. Usually when a large ship is at sea the officers devote a period in the late afternoon to strenuous topside games; they heave medicine balls, play a rough and vigorous game known as "bull-in-the-ring," or rig up a net and play deck tennis.

The newly-commissioned ensign normally serves some seven years at sea and wins promotion first to lieutenant (junior grade) and then to lieutenant, before serving his first tour of duty ashore. Thereafter the usual tours (to which there are, however, many exceptions) are three years afloat and two years ashore, though for senior ranks the tour of sea duty decreases to two years, or even one year.

In type and variety shore duty varies from the desk duty of Washington, where all officers in the Navy Department wear civilian clothes, to the governorship of Guam. (Both Guam and Samoa are administered by the Navy and governed by naval officers.) The officer may live in government quarters, or he may be given an allowance for rent. In his life ashore the officer tends to mix considerably more with civilians than it is possible for him to do when he has duty afloat, but, even so, naval officers tend to move more in cliques of their own kind, "to stick to themselves," more than do army officers.

The officer has the privileges of rank but its responsibilities, too. He must make decisions, quickly and accurately, upon which may depend the lives of men. The captain is responsible for the safety of his ship under any and all circumstances; if something happens to that ship, no matter whose fault it is, the captain is answerable.

Officers have retirement and pension rights, but they are subject to discipline, just like the enlisted man. They can be tried by general court-martial (though not by deck, or summary courts-martial, which are for enlisted men only); they can be "put under hack" (confined to their quarters) by their skipper (who is also known as the "old man") without any ceremony whatsoever; they can be reprimanded, dismissed from the service, imprisoned, or even—for heinous crimes—sentenced to death.

The rules and regulations for officers' conduct and the written and unwritten "don'ts" which hedge in an officer's life fill pages in *Naval Regulations*, but perhaps the most popular, concise, and at the same time common-sense rules of behavior for a naval officer are to be found in the verses, *The Laws of the Navy*, by Captain Hopwood, R.N. These verses, which follow in very much abridged form, have long been the channel buoys by which young officers have navigated through the

shoals of naval life, and every plebe entering the Naval
Academy has had to learn them by heart.

"Now these are the laws of the Navy,
     Unwritten and varied they be:
And he that is wise will observe them,
     Going down in his ship to the sea;

As naught may outrun the destroyer,
     Even so with the law and its grip,
For the strength of the ship is the Service
     And the strength of the Service, the ship.

"Take heed what ye say of your seniors,
     Be your words spoken softly or plain,
Lest a bird of the air tell the matter,
     And so ye shall hear it again.

"If ye labour from morn until even'
     And meet with reproof for your toil,
It is well—that the guns be humbled,
     The compressor must check the recoil.

"On the strength of one link in the cable,
     Dependeth the might of the chain.
Who knows when thou mayest be tested?
     So live that thou bearest the strain:

.   .   .   .

"Now these are the Laws of the Navy
     And many and mighty are they.
But the hull and the deck and the keel
     And the truck of the law is—OBEY."

But the officer, if he is a good officer, has learned the lesson of obedience as a plebe or in the Naval Reserve; indeed, some critics think that given the Navy's present system of promotion, there has been too much emphasis upon strict obedience of higher authority and not enough upon initiative.

The system of promotion, schooling, and pay is complicated but precise and extensive.

A warrant officer, who, in the stilted vernacular of the service, ranks "with but after an ensign," is neither fish nor fowl; he is not an enlisted man and he is not a commissioned officer. All ranks from ensign and above hold commissions from the President; a warrant officer, as his title implies, merely holds a warrant, though a chief warrant officer is that anomalous creature, a "commissioned-warrant" officer. The various ranks in the Navy, with their designating insignia, illustrated on page 84, are listed below. The gold stripes of rank—gold braid surmounted by the special corps device or warrant-officer insignia—are worn around the sleeves of the blue uniform, near the cuffs. When white uniforms are worn the shoulder straps denote the rank. Officers' uniforms in the Navy are the familiar double-breasted navy-blue blouse with brass buttons, the navy-blue slacks; white collar and shirt with black tie; black socks and shoes; and cap with visored brim, the insignia of rank and the eagle upon it. Senior ranks, from commander up, wear caps whose brims are encrusted with golden filigree work (the more gold the higher the rank); hence the term "brass hats." White uniforms are white slacks;

white socks and shoes; the blouse with the high, buttoned-up standing collar, brass buttons, and shoulder straps. Dress uniforms run a gamut of styles from frock coats to "tails" and are variously adorned with epaulettes, dress, gilt-fibered sword belts, cocked hats or "fore-and-afters," etc.

INSIGNIA OF RANK

RANK	SLEEVE MARKINGS	SHOULDER STRAP MARKINGS
Warrant Officer (Gold lace is woven at 2-in. intervals with dark-blue silk 1/2 in. thread.)	1/4 in. gold stripe	On black background same width and type of stripes
Chief Warrant Officer (Gold lace is woven at 2-in. intervals with dark-blue silk 1/2 in. thread.)	1/2 in. gold stripe	Same as sleeve
Ensign	One 1/2 in. gold stripe	One 1/2 in gold stripe
Lieutenant (junior grade)	One 1/2 in. gold stripe with one 1/4 in. stripe above it	Same as sleeve
Lieutenant	Two 1/2 in. gold stripes	Same as sleeve
Lieutenant Commander	Two 1/2 in. stripes with one 1/4 in. stripe between	Same as sleeve

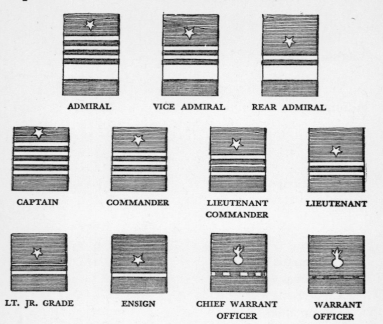

ADMIRAL VICE ADMIRAL REAR ADMIRAL

CAPTAIN COMMANDER LIEUTENANT COMMANDER LIEUTENANT

LT. JR. GRADE ENSIGN CHIEF WARRANT OFFICER WARRANT OFFICER

Sleeve Markings Showing Rank of Naval Officers with Corps Devices Above; Stars Are for Line Officers; Flaming Stars for Gunners

RANK	SLEEVE MARKINGS	SHOULDER STRAP MARKINGS
Commander	Three ½ in. stripes	Same as sleeve
Captain	Four ½ in. stripes	Same as sleeve
Rear Admiral	One 2 in. stripe with one ½ in. stripe above it	Anchor with two stars on background of gold lace

RANK	SLEEVE MARKINGS	SHOULDER STRAP MARKINGS
Vice-Admiral	One 2 in. stripe with two ½ in. stripes above it	Anchor with three stars, etc.
Admiral	One 2 in. stripe with three ½ in. stripes above it	Anchor with four stars, etc.

From ensign to admiral in the Navy corresponds roughly, as follows, with army ranks:

NAVY	ARMY
Ensign	Second Lieutenant
Lieutenant (J.G.)	First Lieutenant
Lieutenant	Captain
Lieutenant Commander	Major
Commander	Lieutenant Colonel
Captain	Colonel
Rear Admiral (Junior)	Brigadier General
Rear Admiral (Senior)	Major General
Vice-Admiral	Lieutenant General
Admiral	General

The rank of Commodore which roughly corresponded to what are now the junior officers on the rear admirals' list was, for a long time, a permanent rank in the Navy, but it has been abolished, and there remain only seven commodores on the retired list. However, the title is sometimes applied unofficially and slangily to the "old man" or captain commanding a squadron of destroyers.

The distribution of officers in the various grades is fixed by law and is about as follows:

Rear Admiral 1%
Captain 4%
Commander 8%
Lieutenant Commander 15%
Lieutenant 30%
Lieutenant (junior grade) and Ensign .. 42%

Permanent promotions in our peacetime Navy are made only to the rank of rear admiral. There are four positions, such as chief of naval operations; commander in chief of the Pacific Fleet; commander in chief Atlantic Fleet; commander in chief Asiatic Fleet, which carry with them temporary promotion to full admiral; there are a few other jobs which carry with them temporary promotion to vice-admiral. But the incumbent, as soon as he is relieved of that position, reverts to his permanent rank of rear admiral as long as he remains on the active list of the Navy. When he retires, a former chief of naval operations is now entitled, under the law, to retire with the rank of full admiral.

The approximate *average* pay for line officers and their equivalent in the staff corps is given in the following table:

RANK	AVERAGE YEARLY PAY
Ensign	$1,500
Lieutenant (junior grade).......	2,137
Lieutenant	2,942
Lieutenant Commander	4,138

RANK	AVERAGE YEARLY PAY
Commander	5,046
Captain	5,994
Rear Admiral	7,198

The above figures include the base pay in each grade plus the 5 per cent three-year longevity increases. There are other allowances which increase these figures somewhat—entertainment and special allowances for senior officers like captains and admirals. There is also a differential in rental and subsistence allowance between married and unmarried officers. Officers with dependents when not occupying Government quarters receive an average rental allowance of about $1,012. Officers without dependents receive a similar average rental allowance of $639. The rental allowance increases with rank; these figures are the average for all grades. Average subsistence allowance is more than $500 for officers with dependents, about $219 for officers without dependents. Aviators receive an increase of 50 per cent of their base pay, not to exceed an extra $1,440 annually; officers on submarine duty receive an extra 25 per cent.

All officers must retire at the age of 64; they may apply for voluntary retirement after 30 or 40 years' service, or they may be retired for physical disability at any time. Officers receive retired pay in proportion to their length of service and the base pay they are receiving at the time of retirement. An officer may retire with a maximum of 75 per cent of his base pay (less subsistence and rental) as in the case of a captain retiring after 35 years' service, or as low as 24 per cent of his base pay in the case of Lieutenant (junior grade), retiring after 14 years' service.

The ranks and pay of officers of the Marine Corps correspond generally with the army ranks and pay scales. The titles, designations, and insignia—except for the uniforms and the distinctive corps insignia of the Marine Corps—are the same. Marine officers are also liable to duty ashore or afloat; the larger number of them are ashore, officering the Fleet Marine Corps units, in charge of Marine Guards at various places, etc. In land warfare their jobs correspond closely to those of army officers of similar grade, except that the marine must have a greater knowledge of amphibian operations and must master the details of landing on an enemy shore. Afloat the marine officer must be prepared to stand a deck watch in port, and to take charge of the fire of a broadside battery during action or target practice. Marines, however, are assigned only to the larger ships, battleships and cruisers, and form the cadre of the landing parties from those ships whenever landing parties are necessary.

The Navy's officer corps is divided into line and various staff corps. The regular line officers are the backbone of the Navy; they perform general duties of any character ashore and afloat. The specialists of the staff corps, like doctors, dentists, and chaplains, have certain military duties (the paymaster, for instance, may be a member of a decoding board, in action) but are primarily specialists. Warrant officers are still a third and special class of specialists, qualified for their particular jobs, but not for general duties. Line officers are the only ones who can command afloat; they are the combat branch of the officers' corps which the other corps serve.

Of Regular Navy officer personnel on active duty October 1, 1941, 7,511 were line officers; 1,069 were in the medical corps; 321 were in the dental corps; 609 were in the supply corps; 104 were in the chaplain corps; 133 were in the civil engineer corps; 990 were chief warrant officers; and 1,059 were warrant officers. The former construction corps of the Navy was abolished recently and its 214 members made line officers for engineering duty only.

Line officers can be at once distinguished from officers of the other corps by the gold star they wear above the stripes on their sleeves, or on their shoulder straps. The other corps wear the device of their corps—a cross for the chaplains, etc.—in a similar position in place of the star. Warrant officers wear the insignia of their particular specialty—such as a propeller for a warrant machinist—in place of the star.

Officers of the line of the Navy may be assigned to nearly any position, afloat or ashore; on small ships such as destroyers, where there is no room for a supply officer or paymaster, they even take over the accounts, act as commissary officer, and when on detached duty or isolated (up the Yangtse River, for instance) they even pay the men.

Young line officers, when they are first ordered to a ship of the Navy, are usually assigned as junior officers of departments and divisions by the executive officer, or second-in-command of the ship, although the executive officer frequently allows division officers to help in the selection.

The captain of a ship of the Navy is called captain regardless of his rank. He may actually have the rank of captain in a battleship or cruiser, or he may be only a lieutenant commander or lieutenant in a destroyer or submarine, but he is the captain, the old man, the high and mighty of that particular ship. His executive officer, usually with the rank of commander in the case of big ships, is the second-in-command. He corresponds to the general manager; he runs the administrative and organizational details of the ship, and, under the direction of the captain, he has full charge of all matters relating to personnel, routine, and discipline.

In any ship there are usually five main line departments, each of which is divided into divisions, with sometimes four or five staff or auxiliary departments. The heads of departments are usually ordered specifically to this duty and are responsible to the executive officer and to the captain.

The navigator is the head of the navigation department, a small but important department, which is concerned with compasses, chronometers, sextants, and all the paraphernalia of navigation. The navigator is responsible for the safe navigation of the ship.

The gunnery officer is the head of the gunnery department, usually the largest of the ship, and is responsible for all ordnance equipment aboard, such as guns, torpedo tubes, etc., and for the training of all gun and torpedo crews.

The first lieutenant and damage control officer is responsible for the cleanliness and upkeep of the ship and for her watertight integrity; he is concerned with watertight doors and hatches, with knowledge of how to equalize a list, etc. The engineer officer is in charge of the ship's propelling machinery and the auxiliaries. The communications officer is in charge of the ship's communication system: radio, sound, and visual.

Watch and division officers are in each case assistants to the heads of the main departments and command units of those departments; for instance, each turret aboard a battleship is manned by one division which is commanded by a division officer who in action has charge of that turret. These officers stand periodic watches or tours of duty in port and underway. Some of them may be on the quarter-deck or the bridge, as officers-of-the-deck, others in the engine room or fire-rooms, others in the radio room or communication office.

All the heads of departments and watch and division officers are line officers. In larger ships heads of departments are usually commanders or lieutenant commanders, occasionally lieutenants; in smaller ships, such as a destroyer, the executive officer may also be navigator; two jobs may be merged in one man; department heads may be lieutenants. Watch-standers and division officers range in rank from ensigns to lieutenant commanders, depending upon the size of the ship and the job's responsibility. The frequency of the tours of duty or watches depends in large measure upon the qualified watch-standers available; it may be only one four-hour watch in eight or twelve on a battleship; it may be one in three on a destroyer.

Other departments are auxiliary to the major ones; the medical officer and dental officer head obviously necessary departments which are splendidly equipped with operating tables, dental chairs, anesthetics, and the finest in instruments and medicines. The supply officer has charge of the general mess, the ship's store, pay accounts, provisions, clothing, and general stores; the chaplain has general welfare, religious, and entertainment duties. The marine officer is in command of the marines aboard, and although he rarely stands the watch of an officer of the deck, except sometimes in port, he has command of a number of the guns in a broadside battery. The senior aviator has charge of the planes aboard.

A young line officer, leaving Annapolis, is more or less on probation for two years after graduation, and if he shows himself a good officer during that period his commission becomes permanent.

Officers are given detailed efficiency reports by their seniors no matter on what station or ship they may serve. These efficiency reports, together with other records of the officer's career—excellent gunnery scores, letters of commendation or censure, courts-martial, if any, etc.—form the officer's record, and it is this record which is examined periodically when officers are selected for promotion.

An ensign who gets his permanent commission automatically becomes a lieutenant (junior grade) after three years' service, but from then on a board of nine senior

officers, known as a selection board, reviews the records
of all officers who are eligible for promotion and se-
lects for promotion all those it feels are qualified. In
each grade, an officer must complete at least four years'
service including two years' sea service. There are only
a certain number of vacancies in each grade and these
vacancies decrease in number the higher the grade, so
that while the selective process eliminates relatively
few in the junior grades, very few can be selected for
promotion in the higher grades. Natural processes of
attrition, physical defects (an officer must have a physical examination every year), deaths, resignations (officers can and frequently do resign from the service,
though resignations are rarely accepted in periods of
emergency), and other causes add to the attrition. Those
who are not selected for promotion have another
opportunity for selection later, and if they are again
"passed over" they may serve in the same grade for a
certain period before enforced retirement. When selected for promotion an officer must pass both mental
and physical examinations and if he successfully passes
these he must wait until there is a vacancy in the next
higher grade above him when he "makes his number"
and pins on the new shoulder straps of increased rank
and responsibility.

The system of promotion is thus competitive, and
though not always fair in the case of certain individuals,
it eliminates the slow and deadening process of promotion by seniority and does put a premium upon
efficiency.

The Navy's system of officer schooling is similarly

strenuous. The Naval Academy is only the first step in it.

The officer is graduated from the Academy with the basic fundamentals of the "jack-of-all-trades" that he must be in his mind; aboard ship he learns more—much, much more, and develops the practical application of the theory he has learned. And while, if he stays in the line of the Navy, he must always keep himself competent to take any post from engineering officer to communication officer, he early starts to find the type of professional work for which he is best qualified, be it gunnery, communications, or engineering, and then starts specializing in it.

There are many officers' schools for the study of specialized subjects, but there are also general schools where the naval officers' education can be extended and broadened. One such is the Naval Postgraduate School at Annapolis, where young officers who have had sea experience return to broaden their general professional and allied knowledge and to commence specialization in certain topics. Later the specialists are generally sent for a further one or two-year course of instruction to outstanding civilian institutions specializing in the particular subject which the student is learning. One hundred and two officers, line, staff and marine corps, received such specialized instruction at places like Massachusetts Institute of Technology during the 1940 fiscal year. Subjects studied include everything from ballistics to marine engineering and aerography. Some students are sent abroad for instruction; before the war they were to be found in the great universities of Europe,

and even in 1940 nineteen naval and marine officers
were studying Chinese, Japanese, Russian, or Spanish
abroad.

Other naval officers, who after their requisite period
of duty afloat, wish to specialize in aviation, are sent
to Pensacola for a year's flight training if they can pass
super-rigid physical examinations. These officers are
given their wings upon completion of the course, and
from then on throughout most of their naval career
they are assigned to duty involving flying, remaining
naval aviators so long as they are qualified for such duty,
physically and otherwise. But they are naval officers,
too, and must pass examinations in all naval subjects;
the Navy insists that its pilots, like its engineers and
navigators, must be general all-round naval officers first,
and specialists second.

The schools in some form or another continue
throughout most of a naval officer's career if that officer
wants to take advantage of them, as he usually does.
There is a torpedo school at Newport, Rhode Island, a
submarine school at New London, Connecticut, for
training new submarine officers, and various courses at
Army schools. The most important and ultimate school
for any naval officer who aspires to high command is
the Naval War College at Newport, Rhode Island,
where junior, senior, and advanced courses are given.

It is here that the science and art of fleet handling is
taught on the great game board, where models of ships
and planes are moved about by opposing commanders;
it is here that the strategy of naval warfare is learned
by intensive study. And it is here—in the library, in the

study, and on the game board—that history teaches its living lessons, and that the officer learns in theory what he later applies in practice in the fleet—the tremendous, the difficult, the fascinating job of handling and leading men, of co-ordinating the operations of different types and classes of ships and planes, of welding the disparate elements of Sea Power into a unified, effective whole.

CHAPTER FOUR

THE FIGHTING SHIPS

THE power and glory and majesty of a nation are epitomized in her Fleet. The great gray ships that ride upon the waters, the great ships that so few Americans ever see, may indeed stand between us and the ancient wrongs. The Fleet is the first pillar of American security, and it must be strong.

The Fleet is composed of many different elements and of various types, some of them so diverse as to offer tremendous difficulties in co-ordinated operations. There are the main combatant vessels of the Fleet; there are specialized types for particular operations such as minelaying; there are the auxiliaries, such as tenders, store ships, oilers, which exist to service the Fleet; and there are the unromantic, trudging merchantmen, the liners and cargo vessels, which in time of war may become auxiliary cruisers, transports, or supply ships.

The five principal combat types in any first-class navy are battleships, aircraft carriers, cruisers, destroyers, and submarines. Each of these types is in turn divided into class groups according to their characteristics; the battleships, *New York* and *Texas,* are sister ships with only relatively small differences, and they were built about the same time from the same designs; hence they are of the same *class.* Carriers may be large or small; cruisers may be light or heavy; destroyers and submarines may be of many different classes.

The characteristics—speed, gun power, tonnage, cruising radius, armor, etc.—of a fighting ship vary widely, depending upon the purpose or mission for which the ship was built, the stage of advancement of engineering and scientific knowledge at the time of construction, the efficiency of a nation's steel mills, gun factories, and shipyards, and particularly the nature of the country's naval problem. A nation like the United States, for instance, with coastlines on two great oceans, requires fighting ships with great cruising radii which can operate far out in those oceans.

Though the detailed characteristics of ships of different nations vary widely, as any reference to *Jane's Fighting Ships,* the big and popular reference book of the world's navies, will show, battleships all over the world have certain qualities in common and so do cruisers and destroyers and the rest.

BATTLESHIPS

BATTLESHIPS and battle-cruisers are sometimes grouped together and called *capital* ships, a designation first officially used in the Washington Naval Limitation Treaty of 1921–22, which restricted sizes and characteristics of the world's fighting ships for some fourteen years until it was abrogated by Japan. But battle-cruisers, of which there are only a few in the world's navies and none in the United States Navy, should not be confused with cruisers. Battle-cruisers are as big or bigger than battleships; they are faster but they are not as heavily armored. As a type they are disappearing because advances in marine engineering have enabled modern battleships to attain speed without sacrificing protection.

A battleship is a big-gunned, heavily armored, big ship, which is still considered by all first-class navies to be the principal unit or type of fighting ship. A number of battleships make up a navy's battle line; upon the strength of that battle line depends in large measure the ultimate strength of that navy.

The battleship epitomizes power, the ability to stand and slug and take it; a battleship, as *The Bluejackets' Manual* says, is designed "to fight any vessel anywhere." A battleship, like any other ship ever built or ever to be built, can be sunk, but it is believed to be the least vulnerable type and is designed to withstand shell hits, bomb hits, torpedoes, and mines.

In May, 1941, the German battleship *Bismarck* was struck by a minimum of six, a maximum of ten, torpedoes and was hit by innumerable shells, yet shortly before she finally foundered, the Commander-in-Chief, British Home Fleet, radioed: "Can't get her to sink with guns."

By most naval officers battleships are considered the backbone of the Fleet; when Fleet meets Fleet the guns of the battleships are the ultimate arbiters of the action.

They are the tactical center of a fleet; around them the smaller types maneuver.

The United States today has seventeen battleships, the oldest the *New York, Texas,* and *Arkansas* (of the Atlantic Fleet), which are limited in gun range to about 22,000 yards because their big guns can be elevated only 15 degrees; the newest the *North Carolina* and *Washington,* each armed with nine sixteen-inch guns and completed only recently. Fifteen other battleships have been contracted for, although the keels of eight of them have not yet been laid. The *North Carolina* and the *Washington* are the world's most modern capital ships and are probably superior in fighting characteristics to the new *King George V* class of Britain or the *Littorio* class of Italy. Less is known about the German *Tirpitz,* sistership of the *Bismarck,* or the two Japanese battleships that are expected to be put in commission late this year or early in 1942.

The *North Carolina,* pride of the new American Navy, displaces about 35,000 tons of tough fighting steel at normal standard load, 40,000 tons or perhaps more at full load. She has a beam of 108 feet, sufficient to give her a one-foot clearance on either side when she is put through the locks of the Panama Canal. Her draft is more than thirty feet.

The new ship is a long, sleek, two-stack vessel, armed with nine sixteen-inch 45 caliber guns (caliber, when used in reference to naval guns, is a measure of the length of the gun expressed in terms of the gun's diameter; *viz.,* a 45 caliber gun is 45 times 16 inches long

or 60 feet long). These guns are arranged in what are
known as triple turrets—three to a turret, with two turrets or heavy-armored gun housings forward, and one
aft. The guns weigh about 125 tons apiece and each
turret with its three guns weighs about 1,100 tons.

The combined double-purpose guns of the secondary
battery are five inches in size and there are twenty

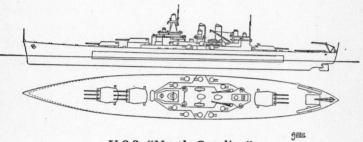

U.S.S. "North Carolina"

of them, mounted in ten high-angle double turrets.
There are in addition numerous .50 caliber machine
guns and 1.1-inch "hose" guns for antiaircraft purposes.

The *North Carolina* is heavily armored. There are
several protective, or armored decks, and her side
armor is at least sixteen inches thick at vital points,
tapering down forward and aft. She has triple below-
water skins and interior "blisters" or compartments to
take the shock of explosion. She is cut up into many
watertight compartments, like a honeycomb, so that if
one is flooded, the ship will not sink. Four planes are
carried aft.

The *North Carolina* is able to concentrate on a target fifteen to eighteen miles away more than eighteen heavy shells, or twenty tons of steel and T.N.T., every minute.

But one of the most amazing things about her is her speed. In comparison with our present battleships, the fastest of which can make less than 22 knots,

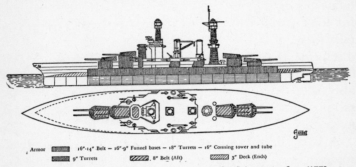

Armor ▓▓▓ 16"-14" Belt — 16"-9" Funnel bases — 18" Turrets — 16" Conning tower and tube
▓▓▓ 9" Turrets   ▨▨ 8" Belt (Aft)   ▨▨ 3" Deck (Ends)

Distribution of Armor on a Battleship of the "West Virginia" Class

the *North Carolina* has a designed speed of 27 to 28 knots and it is expected that she will do more before her trials are finished. Driving her four great propellers are turbines spun by steam, steam heated in oil-burning boilers and compressed to pressures and temperatures probably unprecedented for battleship use in any navy. The weight of her new engine plant has been cut, despite its power, by some 400 tons as compared to plants which operate on low-pressure, low-temperature steam, and this saving has gone into increased protection. Welding, instead of riveting, has been used where possible to make further savings.

She has cost more than $65,000,000 (perhaps a good bit more) as compared to the $27,000,000 per ship which the *Maryland* class cost.

But if you examine a battleship, particularly a modern battleship—which is the most complex thing the mind of man has yet devised—you will understand why.

A battleship is a floating city and a floating fort, a home for 1,500 men, equipped with facilities adequate for long periods to sleep and quarter, feed and entertain them, to take care of them when they are sick, to discipline them, to supply them with plenty of water for washing and drinking (and the American sailor probably uses twice as many gallons a day as the average sailor of any other navy), but above all able to fight and keep on fighting.

A battleship has usually a long-sweeping top deck, sometimes on the same level for the entire length of the ship, sometimes broken into two levels. This deck is covered with teak, a hard tropical wood, which the sailors scrub white. Out of it rise the masts and funnels and what is known as "superstructure," the topside bridgework and other structures which reach above the deck. Out of it, too, rise the huge bulky turrets out of which the main battery guns protrude like reaching fingers of steel. The turrets are great, heavily armored forts which hold the guns, and are mounted on rollerpath bearings on top of huge steel barbettes, or cylindrical structures of armored steel which extend vertically down to below the water line opening at the bottom into the lower handling room and the magazines.

Powder and shell are lifted from the lower handling room by means of mechanical conveyors to the guns, but they must pass through several different compartments and stages, each screened off from the other by flameproof hatches, as they go up. A conning tower with eighteen inches or more of armor, is generally directly forward of the foremast and is the place from which the captain controls or "conns" the ship in action.

The foremast on modern battleships (*North Carolina*) is a cone-shaped steel structure, with bridges built up around its lower portion and with light antiaircraft guns mounted around it. A heavily armored tube, housing electric control cables, leading from the director and other fire-control instruments which are situated near the top of the mast, leads down into the bowels of the ship, to the plotting room, where the ranges to be set upon the guns are worked out. Some of our battleships —the three *Maryland* class and the *Tennessee* and *California*—still have the old-type cage masts which were once a distinguishing feature of United States ships, but our older battleships which have been modernized, or rebuilt, have replaced these masts, in most instances, with tripods, which are steadier, or with a built-up mast.

One of the most expensive items in a battleship's construction is fire-control apparatus; that is electromechanical apparatus of a highly technical type used to control the fire of the guns. Machines that integrate and calculate and do everything but live and breathe, delicate and expensive machines that, figuratively, "can

put a shell on a dime at 10,000 yards" are everywhere
on a modern warship. Optical and electrical instruments
of many kinds are other items of major cost.

Nearly everything you can think of, and many you
couldn't, go into a modern battleship, *viz.:*

20,000-pound anchors	Hydraulic jacks
3,000 feet 3-inch anchor chain	Airplane catapults
250 chairs	Two motion picture projectors
30 typewriters	One piccolo
70 desks	Five clarinets
One electrical bacteriological incubator	Three trombones, etc., for band
Ten electric refrigerators	1,000 portable power and hand tools
Potato peeler	Air whistles
Dishwashing machine	Chronometers
Twelve eighty-gallon steam-jacketed kettles	Bells
One soda fountain	Foghorns
Four sewing machines	Mail boxes
Shoe repair equipment	Printing presses
Six barber chairs	Safes
One portable pulpit	Hammocks
Oxygen rescue breathing apparatus	Steam turbines
Garbage incinerator	Ice-cream freezers, etc.
	Guns of all sizes, etc.

The raw materials for all this cost only about $10,-
000,000 or $11,000,000; the rest is largely labor costs,
the highest-priced labor in the world, with the highest

standards of living, standards of living which these very battleships protect. About 12,000 plans and countless thousands of blueprints, which it takes a couple of trucks to carry, several years to produce, and which cost $3,000,000, are the battleship's genesis—the blueprint dream which in the slow travail of the shipyard finds final realization, after four years of birth pangs, in the mightiest type afloat.

AIRCRAFT CARRIERS

THE principle of construction of all armored ships—whether battleship or cruiser—is the same. The vital parts of the ship, the parts that must be preserved from too severe damage if the ship is to go on fighting and steaming, are enclosed in a so-called "armored citadel," formed by turrets and barbettes, deck and side armor.

A water-line belt of heavy armor, which varies in height and thickness depending on the type and on the ship, usually extends from forward of the forward group of magazines to aft of the after group; and the ends of this belt are connected athwartships by armored bulkheads. The turrets revolve within and above the armored, cylindrical barbettes which extend beneath the protective deck. The protective deck, or decks (the lighter protective deck is usually called the "splinter" deck), covers the engine room, boiler rooms, plotting room, and the lowest is usually just above the water line.

This same principle is followed in those of our aircraft carriers which are armored. Not all are armored. The *Ranger*, for instance, one of six now in commission (twelve others are building) is unarmored. Despite armor, aircraft carriers are vulnerable to gunfire, and they are not intended to be gun platforms, which is

Aircraft Carrier "Wasp"

the main function of most fighting ships, or to fight with their guns. For the plane is their weapon.

Carriers, sometimes known to the Navy as the "covered wagons" of the ocean, are simply mobile landing fields of the sea. Their flat-topped decks give them a distinctive and odd appearance, since their upper deck is as level as a tennis court and they have no superstructure except a single "island" of bridge, control stations and mast being set way over to one side of the deck. The smoke stacks (known in the Navy as "stacks") are also set to one side, and are sometimes folding.

The flight deck itself is long and provides ample space to practiced aviators for landing a plane, or for taking off. The carrier is underway, steaming at various speeds and heading into the wind when the planes take off, and thus the ship's speed—which "creates" a wind, is added to the force of the actual breeze to aid the take-offs. Thus, if there is a fifteen-mile breeze blowing and the carrier is making fifteen knots, the planes will be lifted quickly from the flight deck by a wind of more than thirty miles an hour.

The normal complement of an American carrier is seventy-eight operating planes—four squadrons plus a few utility planes (plus some 25 to 50 per cent reserves carried partially disassembled), and all four squadrons, usually of eighteen planes each, can take off and clear the carrier's deck in as little as eighteen to thirty minutes.

Landings are somewhat slower; the homing planes circling over the carrier are flagged down in turn, and their landing directed by an officer on the ship's stern. The planes "pancake" down; hooks which are lowered from the fuselage catch in one of seven wires stretched a few inches high athwartships across the flight deck, and the plane is stopped quickly as the wires, held on each end by hydraulic brake drums, check the plane's forward progress uniformly and without a great jerk. Two plane elevators can lower the planes to a great cavernous hangar deck below.

The main weapon and the only reason for a carrier is its brood of planes, but all carriers also carry antiaircraft guns, some of them in great number; and all of them are armed with a main battery of five to eight-inch guns. These guns are usually emplaced on platforms set out from the flight deck, or in turrets or gun housings to one side of the flight deck. Some of our carriers have light armor belts, but their decks of wood are their vulnerable point, and their planes and their speed, varying from 29 to 34 knots, are their real defense. They carry crews of from 1,400 to 1,900 men.

A carrier's job is to give punishment but not to take it. In a fleet action its position is out of sight beyond the horizon—perhaps 30 to 100 miles from the battle line, safe from the fire of enemy guns. A carrier's planes are its guns, with ranges of several hundred miles, and a carrier's first objective in a fleet action is the enemy's carriers; second, its battle line.

Carriers are also suited to semi-independent operations, although they should always be accompanied by a screen of destroyers or cruisers to guard them against torpedo attack and to act as "plane-guard vessels" in case the carrier's planes fall into the sea. They have long been the principal component of the so-called carrier striking group, a force consisting of a high-speed carrier, and generally two or more cruisers, and possibly some destroyers capable of far-ranging operations against an enemy's commerce, coastline, or detachments of his fleet.

Before this war started it had been thought that carriers would be very vulnerable to attack from land-based aircraft and that they could not usefully be employed—except briefly on daring raids—in narrow waters or close to an enemy coast. But the British carriers have operated successfully off Norway and France, and in the Mediterranean, and until late 1941 none had yet been sunk by air attacks. Some of their safety they unquestionably owe to aircraft warning devices, which operate on the radio-wave principle, and with which American ships of all principal types are being equipped. These devices give warning, in ample time, of an impending air raid by an enemy and permit the carrier to get her planes into the air to intercept it.

Our two largest and most famous carriers—the *Lexington* and *Saratoga,* 33,000-ton giants—which have a greater capacity for sustained speed than any other ships in the world, were converted after the Washington Naval Conference of 1921–22 into carriers from half-finished battle-cruisers. About 108 planes have been landed and flown off the flight deck of the *Saratoga* alone, and she has carried from thirty to sixty more in the hangar deck. As planes become larger and heavier, however, carriers—the Navy's mobile airfields—are experiencing more difficulty in handling them.

CRUISERS

In the United States Navy today there are two principal categories of cruisers—light cruisers of various displacement armed with six-inch main batteries, and heavy cruisers, all of about 10,000 tons' displacement, armed with eight-inch main batteries. There are thirty-seven cruisers—the scouts of the fleet—in commission, but there are fifty-four others ordered, some of them of radically new design and of tremendous tonnage and gun power, so big, in fact, that they will not be cruisers in any real sense of the word, but will approximate battle-cruisers.

The cruiser, unlike the battleship which is rugged and of great beam, is long and narrow; the *Wichita*, for instance, is 614 feet long with a sixty-one-foot beam, but only a twenty-foot draft, and she develops more

Cruiser "Brooklyn"

than 100,000 horsepower and has a speed of more than 32 knots.

All of our cruisers are armored but many of them only lightly and none of them, of course, can stand up to the fire of a battleship. They carry crews of from 458 to 888 men each. Our oldest cruisers of the 7,050 ton *Omaha* class are obsolescent by modern standards, though they are excellent sea boats and still serviceable. The newer eight-inch gun cruisers, though often criticized as "treaty tinclads," are rugged ships with great cruising radii and hitting power. One somewhat similar to ours, the British eight-inch gunned *Exeter,* showed she could "take it" in the classic battle with the German pocket battleship, *Graf Spee.* Most of our eight-inch or heavy cruisers have three triple-gunned turrets and eight five-inch antiaircraft guns. They carry four to six seaplanes and two catapults. But the *Brooklyn* class, with fifteen six-inch guns—five triple-gunned turrets, speed and considerable protection and with room in a hangar below the main deck and on two catapults for eight planes (two partially disassembled)—is one of the Navy's most successful designs. These new ships can pump out considerably more than 100 rounds a minute (some of them above 150) from their remarkably accurate six-inch guns. They have new and very precise fire-control instruments and are well protected against air attack with eight five-inch antiaircraft guns. But only in the latter ones of this class are the antiaircraft gunners protected by gun shields; the *Helena's* five-inch "sky" guns are mounted in pairs in cupola-shaped mounts which protect the gunners against splinters, bombing, and strafing attacks. All American ships are to be so equipped, however. The *Brooklyn* class has a thermostat, steam-heated, air-conditioning system; they are good sea boats and can cruise for thousands of miles without refueling.

Our cruisers are essential both for fleet action and for independent operations. When with the fleet they act as the screen or outer protective force for the main body; they also act as scouts—particularly the big eight-inchers—to discover the enemy's whereabouts. The six-inch gun cruisers are excellent, because of their great rapidity and volume of fire, for repulsing an enemy destroyer attack.

Independently, our cruisers can be used with carriers in far-ranging operations, or alone, to prey upon enemy commerce lanes, for patrol, or to escort our own merchant vessels.

They are in one sense the indispensable jacks-of-all-trades of the ocean highways and since they are protected with armor, perhaps four to eight inches, have considerable speed and great gun power, they are less easy to destroy than a lighter vessel and have considerably more fighting capacity. But they are also more expensive; a modern cruiser may cost from $13,000,000 to $28,000,000.

DESTROYERS

DESTROYERS are the "trouble-boats" of the sea. They are thin, fragile, steel splinters, packed with power, power which racks them from stem to stern, power which gives them greater speeds than any other type of the blue-water fleet. We have about 175 of them—many of them old four-stackers of the World War design—and almost 200 others building. Destroyers are torpedo carriers and gun carriers, as well as depth-charge carriers; they are equipped to hunt submarines (with their underwater listening devices and their "ash cans" or depth charges); or to launch a torpedo attack against an enemy battle line, to escort a convoy, patrol the seas, or to harass commerce. They are unarmored, 37 to 40-knot ships, dependent upon their speed and their maneuverability for their safety. They have relatively shallow drafts, but long cruising ranges and good sea-keeping qualities, though they dance about like a lively lady in a seaway. They are ships of the "dungaree navy"; let's go aboard a typical new one—the streamlined *Hammann*, during her trial run.

The *Hammann* has none of the angular old-maidish appearance of so many ships. The streamlining isn't pronounced, not like the *Normandie*—only rounded deck edges forward on the forecastle and a semicircular bridge structure. It doesn't add much, if anything, to her speed, but strangely enough those rounded deck edges keep the forecastle dry even in rough weather.

The *Hammann* has a large single stack, with curved uptakes from the boiler rooms leading into it, a single pole mast forward, and a searchlight platform rising above the after deckhouse aft.

Come aboard her and stand out of harbor down past Ambrose Light with the sea all about us a calm, scarcely-rippled surface, hung with the haze of morning, lighted now and again by patches of brilliant sunlight.

Faster and faster, but with a ladylike decorum, the *Hammann* dashes over a calm sea. She is live and light as she charges at almost 40 knots past Fire Island, with the sun sparkling on the sea and our course etched in white foam on the blue ocean behind us. There is not much vibration as the huge main throttle is inched open little by little in the engine room and the two great screws flail the water faster and faster.

Above decks the gun muzzles of the *Hammann's* eight five-inchers gleam in the sun and the slim length of her 348 feet seems lean and eager in the sea.

Come below decks and look around.

The officers' staterooms are comfortable, but utilitarian cubicles, with none of the modernistic and somewhat florid effect of rooms aboard French and Italian men-of-war, and with but little of the comfortable, homey appearance of the rooms of British officers. They look just exactly what they are—sea-going hotel rooms, to be used by the officers when they aren't ashore, and they will never look like anything else (for relatively few American officers make their ships their "homes" as British officers do). . . . Bare, painted steel bulkheads. A ventilation system with a shuttered grill which permits entrance into each room of the desired amount of fresh air (heated in cold climates), an electric heater, and a fan; metal furniture—a built-in desk with a little safe and a shaded lamp on a swinging elbow bracket, a light metal chair, a built-in metal bunk with a Beauty-rest mattress, a metal clothes closet and chest of drawers. The skipper's room and the "Commodore's" room, which are high in the mast structure, have their own private baths, an unheard-of luxury in our old four-stacker "tin cans."

But the modern "dungaree navy" has more than one luxury undreamt of in the old fleet of flush-deckers. The navigator on the modern destroyer is virtually a robot (though he must be a thinking robot); a complicated electro-mechanical gadget traces the dead-reckoning course of the vessel in the chart room just back of the

bridge; a fathometer records the ocean depth automatically; a patent log tells the speed; an anemometer,
the direction and force of the wind, a radio loop or
direction finder takes radio bearings and gives the navigator his position in relation to a definite place ashore
or another ship.

The torpedo tubes which fire those $12,000 torpedoes
—or "tin fish" as the Navy calls them—are all controlled
from the bridge. A queer-looking, cupola-shaped dome
structure above two sets of the quadruple mounts gives
protection to the tube trainers against rough seas.

Destroyers, like all other modern men-of-war, have
acquired protective devices of many kinds against the
new menace from the skies. Each of the *Hammann's*
five five-inch guns is capable of high elevation and can
be used against aerial, as well as surface, targets, pump-
ing out some twenty shots a minute. These guns are
also controlled from a central station, and one of the
"hush-hush" features of the *Hammann* class is the plotting room, a brilliantly-lighted room below decks
crammed with electro-mechanical instruments for determining the range of the target. The *Hammann* class
are the first destroyers to be so equipped; heretofore a
plotting room was only for larger vessels like cruisers
or battleships; in previous destroyers the complicated
calculations necessary to determine the range to be set
on the guns was determined from cruder calculations
at the control station, atop the bridge.

But the *Hammann* doesn't depend upon her big guns
alone for antiaircraft defense; she has, or will have, a
considerable battery of heavy machine guns, and her

upper deck is armor plated to deflect machine-gun bul-
lets. If you look up the back files of your newspaper
you will see that the German planes that made the first
attack against the British naval base in the Firth of
Forth, swooped low over British cruisers and destroyers

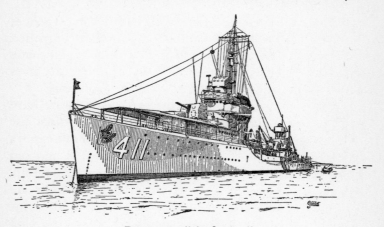

Destroyer "Anderson"

and "strafed" them with machine-gun fire. Long before
the European War started, for that matter, we had used
an old destroyer as a guinea pig in some bombing and
"strafing" experiments on the West Coast, and it was
found that .50 caliber machine-gun slugs cut through
the old steel decks like a knife through cheese and
worked havoc with power leads, electric light cables,
etc. Hence the *Hammann* and most of our new destroyers have thin plates of what is known to the trade as
"special treatment steel" topside.

Speed, of course, is another defensive asset of the

Hammann and her sisters, and against submarines she has depth charges, stowed as usual on the depth-charge racks aft, and a sensitive supersonic underwater listening equipment which can detect at some distance the propeller noises of underwater craft and determine the submarine's approximate whereabouts.

In comfort and habitability the *Hammann* is far ahead of her predecessors. The "deck gang" in the old "tin cans" used to berth forward; the "black gang" or engineers aft, each messing in their own sleeping compartments. In the *Hammann* all the men eat forward in large, light, airy compartments. Mess tables, bolted to the decks, can be cleared after meals and used for recreational purposes. The entire crew sleeps aft in a series of compartments just beneath the main deck. Here, the bunks, folded up out of the way in the daytime, are ranged in tiers three-deep; there are small clothing lockers for each man, and bucket racks with individual locks. Greatest advance are the showers with hot and cold running water, the tiers of washbasins, the ship's laundry, the fine ranges of the galley.

But most spectacular of *Hammann's* equipment is her engineering plant. She is not the first American vessel, by any means, to use the recently developed high-pressure, high-temperature steam installation, but nevertheless she represents the latest of her line, and exponents of progressiveness look upon the *Hammann* design with affectionate pride.

The *Hammann's* boilers develop steam superheated to 725 degrees (850 at the maximum), and cage that steam in asbestos-swathed pipes at 600 pounds' pressure, as compared to the 250 pounds of pressure, the 400 degrees of heat common in naval engineering plants of twenty years ago.

You get some idea of the frightening power contained in steam heated to such temperatures, caged at such pressure, when you see underneath the curved uptakes leading from the three boilers into the stack a heavy steam line looped almost in an S-curve, supported by bulky rollers. It is the line leading from the boiler safety valves below up the stack. Normally cold, the line's expansion is so great when the safety valves lift and the roaring heat of 600 pounds of steam rushes into it that the line straightens out and actually moves several inches on its rollers as the metal is heated by the steam.

Problems such as this—problems of metallurgy—face the engineers and designers who have harnessed and controlled these dynamic energies that are appalling. The boilers, for instance, have to convert 150,000 pounds of water into steam every hour at full power; that steam roars at 150 feet a second through the turbines, impinging against the finely-tempered, razor-thin steel blades, and like wind against the vanes of a windmill forcing the turbine rotor—and through gearing the propeller shaft—to revolve at high speed. Three turbines are used to each propeller shaft—a small cruising turbine employed only at moderate speeds, so small it seems a child's toy—and a high-pressure and low-pressure turbine, weighing eight, and sixteen and a half tons, respectively, and used without the cruising turbine at high speeds. The expansion of the high-pressure steam through the various stages of the turbines, the conversion of its great heat into kinetic energy makes the *Hammann* ride the sea so swiftly.

The plant is a very efficient one—about 28 per cent as compared to the 22 per cent efficiency of the old four-stackers (that is, about 28 per cent of the energy in the raw oil is converted by the boilers and turbines into propulsive power). Efficient—but with peculiar perils. Some officers don't believe that the metallurgists have as yet been able to define adequately the lifetime of metal—such as turbine blading—under such terrific temperatures and strains and stresses as in the *Hammann*. Will the new installation stand up under the test of time? Mr. James K. Davies, the Westinghouse engineer who designed the *Hammann's* turbines, retorts that the *Hammann's* propulsion equipment—mounted on heavy fixtures at the South Philadelphia works of the company—were run at full power and load for eighty hours, the equivalent, he figures, of about ten years' actual service in the vessel (since men-of-war, unlike merchant vessels, are rarely called upon except for a few hours in battle or in maneuvers to run at full speeds).

In the earlier of our new destroyers, like the *Mahan* class, the new high-pressure, high-temperature machinery was crammed into so small a space that the equipment was almost inaccessible to upkeep, overhaul, and repairs; indeed in several instances the ship's side plates had to be removed to reach some equipment. In later destroyers, like the *Hammann,* this situation has been remedied—though even the two engine rooms of the *Hammann* seem to the lay eye a clutter of piping and machinery. Part of this appearance of crowded space is due to the fat steam pipes, so swathed in lagging as to seem thrice their actual size, and yet so hot is the steam that within the swaddling lagging, itself warm to the touch, the bare pipes glow to incandescence.

Such is the destroyer, $8,000,000 sprightly queen of the seas. A destroyer carries a crew of 100 to 200 men, depending on her class.

In the navy of twenty, fifteen, or even ten years ago her chief functions were two—to deliver torpedo attacks against the enemy, and to hunt out and destroy submarines. The latter is still one of her special duties, but today the destroyer is not only valuable because of its torpedo-launching ability, but because of its great volume of antiaircraft fire. Rimmed around the heavier vessels of the fleet or a convoy, as destroyers normally are, they can throw a tremendous volume of hot metal from their double-purpose guns far into the skies. They are useful ships—these destroyers.

SUBMARINES

THE functions of the submarine or "pig-boats" are too well known to require much elaboration. Theirs are the weapons of concealment and surprise; they do not possess either big guns or heavy armor or speed, but they can lurk beneath the waves and with their deadly torpedoes, fired when the submarine is at periscope depth, or even deeper, they can imperil any ship afloat. They can be employed primarily against commerce, as

Germany employs them, or against enemy fleets, as we use them.

Modern submarines may have surface speeds of 19 or 20 knots or even more; submerged they can do no more than nine to eleven knots. They are generally armed with anywhere from six to twelve torpedo tubes, and one three to five-inch gun (plus antiaircraft ma-

Submarine "Salmon" (SS. 182)

chine guns). They carry torpedoes in each tube and 50 to 100 per cent spares. They range in size all the way from the French giant *Surcouf,* bigger than a small light cruiser, to the German 250-tonners. Most of our new ones, like the *Salmon,* have a surface displacement of 1,450 tons (which increases to about 2,198 tons submerged). They have long cruising range—sufficient to operate in the Sea of Japan for some weeks without refueling—and carry a crew of about fifty-five men. They can submerge to depths of 250 or 300 feet (perhaps somewhat more in extreme circumstances) and might stay underwater 24 to 36 hours. They are driven by Diesel engines on the surface, electric batteries when submerged.

In addition to their more conventional and better-known roles, the submarine is an excellent long-distance scout; it can lie off enemy ports to which no surface ship could approach with safety and watch and report upon the movements of the enemy fleet.

They are distinctive black-hulled vessels, their cylindrical pressure hull lying mostly underwater, even when the submarine is on the surface. They have a flat, thin superstructure deck and pressure conning tower, with the "toothpick" of the periscope above it.

We have 105 submarines built, many of them old, and 80 building.

These types are the Navy's principal combat types, but there are many other extremely useful vessels without which no fleet would be complete.

OTHER COMBAT TYPES

ONE of the most spectacular of the newer types is the little motor torpedo boat, such as the PT (Patrol Torpedo) 10 of the British Scott-Paine design, now being built in this country at the Elco works in Bayonne, N. J. These little "mosquito boats," which have adopted as their emblems a Walt Disney design of a fierce mosquito astride a torpedo leaping above an angry sea, are seventy feet long, have a twenty-foot beam, a four-foot draught, and displace 32 tons. They are powered with three Packard, 1,500 horsepower marine engines which drive three screws, and have made speeds above sixty knots. They have made forty knots in fifteen-foot waves. The Scott-Paine design mount four eighteen-inch torpedo tubes (the newer class will mount twenty-one-inch tubes) and four machine guns in power-operated plane turrets. They are of double-planked mahogany, canvas-

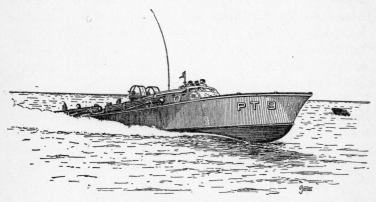

Scott Paine Motor Torpedo Boat

lined construction. They have a variety of uses—for coastal patrol, convoy work, attacks against larger ships (a squadron of twelve boats can approach at sixty knots, fire forty-eight torpedoes in five seconds, turn, and be gone again), and general utility. They are not deep-sea ships in the real meaning of the word, though they have a 1,500 mile radius at twelve knots. They carry their own smoke-making apparatus; can make silent approaches at night with muffled engines, and in their shallow draft and great speeds have characteristics peculiar to their type alone. They are manned by one officer and eight men who wear special windproof and spray-proof clothing and have to have good stomachs and be in splendid physical shape to take the strain of constant vibration and pounding.

Minelayers are generally unarmored ships (sometimes converted merchantmen) with special storage spaces for mines, and deck tracks and gear for launching them over the stern. We have one submarine minelayer with a capacity of some sixty mines and a number of light minelayers, converted from old destroyers, in addition to larger minelayers, and three (including the appropriately named *Terror*) building.

Minesweepers are small vessels, frequently, converted fishing trawlers which do the dirty work of the sea— sweeping up minefields laid by enemies. They are usually of small radius for coastal duty but some few can cruise with the Fleet. They have crews of about seventy-two men each and are equipped with special wires and minesweeping gear.

There are gunboats, like the U.S.S. *Charleston* and *Erie* (20 knots' speed, four six-inch guns, 201 in the crew), patrol vessels of numerous types, submarine chasers, and converted yachts of nearly every description. Scores of these little auxiliary combat craft have been ordered by the Navy Department, and they are indispensable for harbor protection and coastal patrol.

AUXILIARIES

THE Fleet has every kind of auxiliary from transports
to hospital ships; the latter completely equipped with
nearly every kind of medical facility, including nurses,
the only women who go to sea in the Navy! There are
destroyer tenders, with special machine shops for making "floating repairs" to destroyers; there are submarine
tenders, submarine rescue vessels equipped with submarine rescue chambers and decompression chambers
and diving outfits; aircraft tenders with stores of gasoline and oil for the Navy's big patrol planes; light transports (for the marines); net layers for laying and tending
the great nets of steel cable that guard the entrances to
harbors; oilers with supplies of fuel oil for the ships
of the Fleet; supply and store ships, repair ships, tugs,
and countless small harbor craft.

Each of these types and classes has intricate machinery
and equipment of many diverse kinds; indeed the Fleet
is compact of nearly every product of man.

MERCHANT VESSELS

BUT Sea Power, as we have seen, is more than fighting
ships alone. It is also merchantmen, from rust-encrusted
old tramps and our few surviving square-riggers, relics

of the days of sail, to modern liners. Merchant-ship types are even more diverse than are types of fighting ships, but under the "Fifty Ships a Year" program of the Maritime Commission, standardized designs have been worked out, designs in which are incorporated certain military features which make the vessels easily convertible to naval auxiliary use in time of war.

A number of 18-knot tankers (oilers) have been built, some of which already have been taken over by the Navy. They develop 13,500 horsepower and carry tremendous cargoes of oil.

The *Cimarron* class of big tankers are 553 feet overall, have a 75-foot beam, and 23,338 tons' displacement. They have a cruising radius of 10,000 miles. Another and smaller type of tanker being built under the government program is 500 feet long with 68-foot beam, single-screw propulsion, some of them with maximum speeds of 16½ knots.

Liners, like two 759-foot Pacific liners now under contract, have been designed to permit rapid conversion into auxiliary aircraft carriers in war.

The proposed Pacific liners will displace 35,500 tons, will have a designed speed of 24 knots, will be 759 feet overall, with a beam of 98.2 feet. Due to the emergency these fine ships may never be built, but others, like the *America, Manhattan,* and *Washington,* are available for conversion into auxiliary carriers or armed merchant cruisers.

The most numerous class of merchant vessel now being built are cargo ships, and most of these are of the so-called "C-1, C-2, or C-3" types which have the following characteristics:

	C–1	C–2	C–3
Length, feet	413	459	492
Beam	60	63	69.5
Draft	24	25.75	28.5
Horsepower	4,000	6,000	8,500
Speed, knots	14	15.5	16.5
Tonnage (Deadweight)	7,500	8,656	11,975

All these ships, though they have unusually high speeds for cargo vessels, are very efficient and have great cruising radii. Moreover, their decks have been strengthened to permit the emplacement of guns in time of war and they have other naval features.

In addition to these fine designs which would grace any merchant marine in peace two simplified designs have been developed for emergency purposes. One of them, contracted for in great numbers, originally known as the "Ugly Duckling" type is now known as the "Liberty" or EC-L design. These are vessels of simplified design, with designed speeds of 11 knots and a total displacement of 14,100 tons. The other design, as yet unproven, is the radical "Sea Otter," driven by automobile gasoline engines.

Merchant ships of our modern Fleet are truly an important part of the most essential element of Sea Power —ships and shipping.

But there is another element, which in the modern world is no less important—ships of the air, planes.

CHAPTER FIVE

THE FIGHTING PLANES

PLANES, no less than ships, are now an essential element of Sea Power. Planes, no less than ships, now fight the battles of the seas.

The United States Naval Air Service has long been the world's finest naval air arm. It is larger in numbers than any other, better trained, and probably has better pilots. It was the first service in any country to develop dive-bombing, and it also developed our famous bomb sight, the best in the world. But with the entire world now engaged in an air-naval race our Navy will be hard put to it to maintain its lead in the lonely skies above the seas.

The fighting planes of the Navy must have certain characteristics in common with any planes. They must be good flying ships, and they must have good combat characteristics; that is, they must fly as far and as fast as possible; maneuver as handily as possible, climb as rapidly as possible, carry as great a load of bombs and guns and ammunition as possible. But they must also have other characteristics which are not common to land planes.

Their undercarriages (and floats) in particular, and indeed many other parts of their structure, must have greater strength than land planes to withstand the great

129

shocks of landing in a rough sea or against the arresting gear of a carrier, of being flung at sixty miles an hour from a catapult, of roaring in a dive-bombing attack out of the skies at 300 to 500 miles an hour. And their structure and their engines must be constructed insofar as possible to prevent corrosion, for navy planes are constantly exposed to salt spray, wind, and weather. That is one reason why the Navy uses the radial air-cooled engine; it is less susceptible to corrosion and is more accessible to overhaul and replacement. And naval planes cannot be as specialized in function as land planes; they must be capable of doing several jobs and doing them well.

There are four principal categories in the Navy's flying fleets—ship-based planes, patrol planes or flying boats, land-based planes, and lighter-than-air craft. In each of these categories there are various types of planes and there are generally many different models of each type; *viz.*, patrol bombers or flying boats are a type; the Consolidated PBY-5 is a particular model of a patrol bomber. Our Navy until recently did not use the imaginative nomenclature of the British in designating our types and models of planes; instead of a Blackburn Skua or a Swordfish, we prosaically and confusingly called a plane a Grumman F3F-2. An abridged list of the designations and manufacturers' abbreviations used follows:

"V" is a general prefix denoting all heavier-than-air types; "Z" is a similar prefix for lighter-than-air; "X" is a prefix to denote experimental models.

Type Designations		Manufacturers' Designations	
VB	.. Bombing	Brewster	A
VF	.. Fighting	Boeing	B
VO	.. Observation	Curtiss	C
VS	.. Scouting	Grumman	F
VT	.. Torpedo	Martin	M
VP	.. Patrol	Sikorsky, Stearman	S
VN	.. Training	Chance-Vought	U
VOS	.. Observation-Scouting	Consolidated	Y

The numbers between the letters indicate the model; the numbers after the letters the series of the model. Thus VF3F-2—Third Model of the Grumman fighter, modification (or series) two. XF2A-1 is an experimental Brewster fighter, second model, series one.

SHIP-BASED PLANES

SHIP-BASED planes can be carried aboard carriers, aboard the large aircraft tenders like the *Langley,* or aboard battleships and cruisers. No planes are carried aboard smaller ships, though experiments were conducted with a folding-wing plane which fitted into a specially constructed cylindrical deck hangar aboard a submarine, and destroyers have also experimented with plane-carrying.

The carrier-based planes are the real fighting planes of the Fleet's air arm, and they consist of all types. There

are four squadrons, plus a few utility planes (generally
amphibians) and some spares aboard each carrier, and
each squadron usually contains eighteen planes. Generally there is one bombing squadron, one fighting squad-

Vought Scout-bomber. SB2-U-1

ron, one scouting squadron and one torpedo squadron
aboard each carrier. Many of these planes are capable of
doing two jobs; for instance, the torpedo planes can also
carry bombs.

BOMBERS

CURTISS scout-bombers, like the SBC-4, or the newer
XSB2C-1 are dive-bombers. The SBC-4 is a biplane type,
powered with Wright Cyclones, handy and maneuverable. The newer XSB2C-1 is a low-wing all-metal mono-

plane, powered with a 1,700 horsepower Wright Cyclone fourteen cylinder engine. The dive-bomber does

Curtiss Scout-bomber. SBC-4

what its name implies; it approaches its target high in the heavens—with a squadron usually making an approach from four different directions. The pilots stand their planes on "their nose," and dive down at about an 80-degree angle on their target, drop their bombs, and pull out a few hundred or a few score feet above the sea. As the planes "peel off" from their squadron formation high in the heavens and drop like a plummet upon their target, the scream of the wind on their shining surfaces is terrifying. Each dive-bomber may carry as much as half a ton or more of bombs; they have fair speed and considerable range, and can be used as scouts or level-flight bombers.

FIGHTERS

PLANES like the new Grumman mid-wing monoplane with a top well above 300, or the Brewster with a radius of action of 300 to 400 miles are good maneuverable car-

Brewster Fighter. F-2-A-1

rier-based fighters. Both have retractable landing gear and both can carry light bombs in addition to their machine guns. Most carrier-based fighters are not as fast as land-based fighters, but are often more maneuverable and have more range. The great problem is to increase their top speed, without at the same time increasing too much their landing speed, since a high landing speed is dangerous on a carrier deck. The fighters' job is to protect their own carrier, and, of course, to protect their own surface ships against air attack, by knocking enemy planes out of the sky, or preferably, by assisting their own bombers and torpedo planes to sink enemy carriers before his planes can take off.

SCOUTS

MOST of these are dual-purpose planes which can also do dive-bombing, level-flight bombing, or even a little fighting. But the primary job of a plane like the Vought-Sikorsky two-seat scout-bomber with a 700 H.P. Pratt and Whitney engine is maintaining a constant aerial patrol above and ahead of its own carrier, and scouting far ahead of the surface ships to prevent a surprise attack by the enemy.

TORPEDO PLANES

THESE in one sense are the most dangerous of naval air weapons, as the successful British raid on the Italian Fleet at Taranto showed. Planes like the low-wing Douglas TBD-1, powered with 850 H.P. Pratt and Whitney engines, and carrying a crew of three, can transport a 21-inch torpedo, or a considerable bomb load for many hundred miles over the sea. The torpedoes are dropped when the plane is 100 feet or less above the sea's surface, speeding towards the target.

In addition to carrier-based planes which are all wheeled planes, there are other ship-based planes equipped with landing floats and wing floats instead of with wheels. They are the catapult planes, carried aboard battleships and cruisers (three or four to the former, four or six to the latter) for observing and spotting gunfire and for scouting purposes. They are hurled from catapults (powder-actuated in our service) at sixty miles an hour, dip gracefully above the waves, and soar into the heavens.

The spectacle is thrilling but now commonplace and it is no stunt at all to an experienced flier. The plane's propeller is kept turning over as the plane, nested in its cradle, waits to be "shot off." The pilot "revs" her up before the take-off and holds his stick at a fixed angle. He and his observer put their heads back rigidly against the leather headrests to prevent the jerk of the take-off (from zero speed to 60 miles an hour in about 45 feet) from injuring their necks, and the plane is hurled off into the air. When it returns from its flight, it lands in the water, usually in the "slick" or lee formed by the ship, taxies up alongside and is hoisted aboard with a crane. Rough-water landings are spectacular and thrilling and often these seaplanes nose over if they hit a big roller the wrong way. But like all navy planes they are equipped with flotation gear and the pilot, in addition to his parachute, wears an inflatable life-jacket.

Many wing tips are broken and propellers bent by rough weather and by crushing them against the ship's side when being hoisted aboard, but spares are carried, and the proof of effectiveness is in the operations. These little planes take off and land in mid-ocean—sometimes in seas fifteen feet high—and their crews think nothing of it. The Chance-Vought Corsairs, or the Curtiss scout-observation planes are standard for this work; each car-

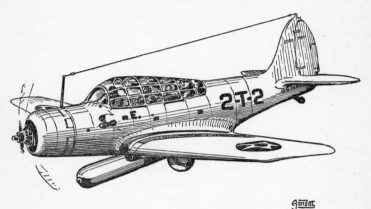

Douglas Torpedo Bomber. TBD-1

ries a pilot and observer; several machine guns and small bombs. They are relatively slow in speed but have considerable cruising range. Those aboard battleships have as their primary mission spotting the fall of shot from the ship's big guns, and radioing back corrections to the ship. Cruiser planes are primarily for scouting purposes, secondarily for spotting.

PATROL PLANES

THESE long-range flying boats are among the most famous and the most effective of the Navy's types. They have flown successfully from San Diego to Panama and from San Diego to Hawaii; models now in service have ranges longer than any of our present land-based planes,

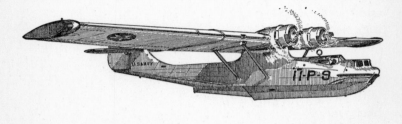

Patrol Bomber (Consolidated). P.B.Y.

and although slower, they can carry an equal or greater weight of bombs. They can stay in the air for thirty or more hours and cover 3,000 to 5,000 miles. They are *boats* that fly; they can live in the open sea and have been refueled in the open sea from surface tenders. They are equipped with bunks, electric stoves, provisions, and an anchor. They skip across the oceans from island to island, and when they pause for rest, they are anchored to moorings laid out by their little surface tenders which precede them. They are not tied to any one land base; they do not need a runway or well-laid-out field; they are in real truth a mobile part of the fleet able to accompany it, to scout for it, and patrol for it far across the seas.

These are the planes which will be stationed from the Aleutians to Panama and from Newfoundland to Trinidad in our island bases. The Consolidated patrol bombers at the moment make up the bulk of the Navy's patrol wings and they are distinctive, among other reasons, because of their retractable wing floats. Most of them are two-engined flying boats, with crews of six to eight men, and speeds of 200 to 220 (but considerably less for cruising, usually 150 to 180); a few four-engined patrol bombers are being ordered of great size, some of which have crews of sixteen, with bunks for eight. The Martin patrol bomber—the PBM-1 and PBM-2—is a new type with two power-operated turrets, six guns—five .50 caliber machine guns and one .30 caliber gun—and a radius of 600 miles with three-ton bomb load.

Patrol bombers can patrol over great areas of ocean, scout for the enemy, and then assist carrier-based, or land-based planes, to bomb him. One patrol bomber can cover 50,000 square miles of sea in one day; they are in real truth the "eyes" of the Fleet.

Some of the newest planes of this type are big amphibians—in effect flying boats equipped with retractable wheels—designed for use in the North, where bays and lakes may be frozen over in the winters.

The patrol squadrons of the Navy's flying fleets are the longest range weapons in the American armory of Mars—in real truth the first line of our first line of defense.

LAND-BASED PLANES

THE Navy, of course, utilizes trainers for its embryo pilots and a great number of various types are now on order. The Naval Aircraft Factory at Philadelphia, only government-owned aircraft factory, makes many of these. The North American NJ-1 advanced trainer, with a weight of 4,470 pounds, powered with a 550 horsepower Pratt and Whitney Wasp engine, is typical. The Navy also uses as trainers some of the same types used with the Fleet, though of older models. The same type plane may be fitted with floats or wheels, so that the student will get amphibian training. The Naval Reserve also generally utilizes wheeled planes—often of the Curtiss scout-observation type—equipped with wheels, instead of floats. Other shore-based planes at naval air stations are amphibian utility planes, which are also utilized aboard carriers.

LIGHTER-THAN-AIR

THE Navy's lighter-than-air activities have not been important since the rigid airships *Akron* and *Macon* were lost, some years after the *Shenandoah* disaster. But the Navy is still training lighter-than-air students at its Lakehurst, N. J., base in the handling of non-rigid, powered blimps, which are extremely useful for coastal patrol and coastal convoy work. They have the ability to remain almost motionless in the air and to take up the speed of a slow surface ship and hence are particularly useful for anti-submarine duties. Forty-eight of these are being ordered for our expanded Navy, and eventually, perhaps another great airship, equipped as a plane carrier, may be ordered.

CHAPTER SIX

EQUIPMENT
AND COMMUNICATIONS

THE standard naval weapon is the gun, but the voice of thunder and the roar of flame with which a sixteen-incher speaks is but symbolic of the power and variety of modern naval arms.

A man-of-war is a maze of machinery and equipment—equipment for fighting and moving, and equipment for signaling and communicating. Rangefinders for taking the distance to the target, rangekeepers—intricate instruments that work out ballistic problems, all sorts of electro-mechanical devices; short-wave radios that can transmit half way round the world or to the next ship in column, these are only a few of the marvelous devices with which a modern fighting ship is chock-a-block.

But the essential strength of a fleet is measured largely by its hitting power. The shell is the principal element of that power, but the torpedo, the bomb, and the mine are highly important weapons of naval war, and the depth charge is an effective anti-submarine weapon.

GUNS AND SHELLS

NAVAL guns are usually designated by their caliber (diameter) in inches, followed by the length of the gun in calibers, followed by a mark and model designation; *viz.*—16 inch 45 caliber, Mark I, Mod. II. They may also be designated by the weight of their projectile, *viz.*, "six-pounder," though this is not usual in the American Navy.

Guns are classified as *turret* guns, *broadside* guns, *antiaircraft, antiaircraft* machine guns, and as *double-purpose* for use against both air and surface targets. Turret guns are the big guns, mounted in armored turrets; broadside guns are the second largest sized guns (usually found only on a battleship) and mounted in small turrets or gun housings or in casemates. The main battery comprises the guns of the largest caliber such as the turret guns; the secondary battery the guns of the next largest size, such as the broadside guns. The big guns or turret guns have as their primary targets the enemy battle line; the secondary battery is usually employed against enemy destroyers, light cruisers, etc.

Guns are constructed in different ways; they are either *built-up* guns; *wire-wound* guns, or *radial-expansion* guns. A *built-up* gun is of different parts and is composed of a liner, tube, and hoops. It is a gun made by shrinking one cylinder of steel over another; the outer cylinder contracting, the inner one expanding, thus locking the component parts together tightly. Most guns in the Navy are of the *built-up* type, and none is of the *wire-wound* type (though the Army uses some), which is simply a gun made by wrapping wire under tension around a cylindrical tube. Radial-expanded guns have been built, up to six inches in size, and they are of monoblock, or single-piece, construction expanded by inside pressure. The *radial-expanded* gun has the advantage of greater strength and less weight. For large guns (up to eight inches) the *built-up* and *radial-expansion* process may be combined.

Guns are rifled to give the projectile the twisting motion which keeps it straight in flight and permits accuracy; and *built-up* guns have liners, or inner cylinders, which can be removed and replaced (at navy yards or shore stations) when worn out. Some guns can be re-lined an indefinite number of times and still preserve their accuracy. Firing a gun produces erosive effects on the steel, which, if enough rounds are fired, becomes of cumulative effect and the gun, or its liner, must be replaced. The number of rounds that can thus be fired, varies with the type of gun, the weight of powder charge used, and the type of construction; four to ten rounds fired with reduced target-practice charges will produce about the same erosion as one service round. The life of a gun is measured by the number of service rounds or its equivalent that it can fire before it loses its accuracy (or has to be re-lined); the life varies—for a sixteen-inch gun it may be 150 to 250 rounds.

The principal sizes of guns with the weight of projectiles used in the United States Navy follow:

3-inch	13 pounds
4-inch	33 pounds
5-inch	50–60 pounds
6-inch	105 pounds
8-inch	250–260 pounds
12-inch	870 pounds
14-inch	1,400 pounds
16-inch	2,100 pounds +

Ships are usually armored in relation to the type of gunfire they are expected to oppose. A battleship armed with sixteen-inch guns is normally armored against sixteen-inch gunfire at battle ranges, which means, roughly, that her armor plate is designed to be of sufficient thickness—about sixteen inches—to resist effectively the penetration of a sixteen-inch shell at 16,000 yards.

The approximate weight of a shell can be determined by the following formula:

Shell's weight equals diameter of gun cubed divided by two, *viz.:*

Weight equals $\dfrac{16 \times 16 \times 16}{2}$, which equals 2,048 pounds, approximate weight of sixteen-inch shell.

Guns use fixed or case ammunition; that is the propelling charge (which explodes in the gun) and the shell are both loaded in a brass cartridge case (like a rifle cartridge); or semi-fixed, in which the propelling charge, but not the projectile, is loaded in a cartridge case; or separate, in which the propelling charge or powder in silk cartridge bags is separately loaded into the gun after the shell is seated. Separate ammunition is used for all big guns; fixed ammunition only for the smaller guns. And it is this powder-bag silk, which burns completely when the gun is fired, for which no effective substitute has yet been found.

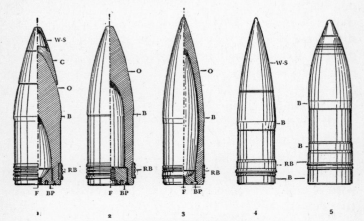

Types of Naval Shells

Various Scales Used for Easy Comparison: 1—12" AP Projectile. 2—6" Projectile. 3—14" Bombardment Projectile. 4—5 Late Design of Projectile with Front and Rear Bourrelets. W-S, Windshield; C, Cap; O, Ogive; B, Bourrelet; RB, Rotating Band; BP, Base Plug; F, Fuse Hole.

Naval projectiles are of several different kinds depending upon the use to which they are put. Target practice projectiles are "duds" or non-explosive shells filled with sand or other material to bring them up to weight. The type most generally used in wartime is armor-piercing, designed to penetrate the heavy armor of an enemy ship. It is a massive piece of steel, and only

a small cavity in its center is filled with the grayish ce-
ment-like substance, cast T.N.T., which is the bursting
charge. In armor-piercing shells only about 2.1 to 2.6
per cent of the total weight of a shell, or about fifty
pounds in a 2,100-pound sixteen-inch shell, is bursting
charge. Common shells have thinner walls and are designed for use against lighter armor or for destructive
damage to superstructures. About 3 to 6 per cent of
their total weight is explosives. High capacity shells are
thin-walled projectiles with as much as 10 to 25 per cent
of their weight in explosives.

All shells are equipped with copper rotating bands
which are gripped by the rifling in the gun and give
the shells during flight their twisting motion. Shells are
usually ogival-nosed; the armor-piercing shell is fitted
with a high-carbon, chrome steel cap to assist penetra-
tive power, and over this cap is fitted a wind shield of
no special strength, but merely designed to streamline
the projectile. A few projectiles, designed for use against
submarines, have flat noses, so that they will not ricochet
from the water. These are sometimes called "diving
shells." Star shells are used at night for illuminating
targets.

Modern guns have great ranges and can be fired extremely rapidly. They can, indeed, be fired further than
their fire can be accurately controlled. At proving-
ground tests guns have been fired 60,000 yards, or more
than thirty miles, without difficulty, but the normal
limit of range for ship-mounted guns is 32,000 to 36,000
yards, and even these ranges, which are usually much
further than people on the firing ship can see, are too

great to expect marked results. Battle ranges for big guns may be between 16,000 and 32,000 yards, depending upon visibility and other conditions.

The secret of accurate gunfire is the control system, or fire-control system, as the Navy calls it, used to control the fire of the guns. The Navy's most modern fire-control devices are carefully guarded secrets and the system is far too intricate, in any case, for description. But briefly it includes rangefinders or optical instruments for taking the distance to the target; directors, usually located high in the ship, from which, by means of a central firing key, all the ship's big guns or main battery may be fired in a thundering broadside (which rocks the ship sideways through the water and sends perhaps nine or ten tons of steel and T.N.T. towards the enemy); telescopes on the guns; rangekeepers and other electro-mechanical instruments for helping to determine the setting for the sights of the guns; and all sorts of electrical transmitting, repeating, and recording instruments.

Our Navy believes that with the help of Sperry, Ford (not the automobile man, but a little firm in Brooklyn), General Electric, and other companies, it has worked out the best fire-control system in the world—one which is almost an automaton. And our seamen are very proud of their gunnery, and indeed when you can put a salvo on a target in short order at a distance of ten to fifteen miles, you have reason to be. For naval gunnery, it must be remembered, is probably more difficult than any other gunnery in the world; you are firing at a tiny sliver of a ship, which perhaps you cannot even see, or at a plane moving at 300 to 400 miles an hour, from a gun platform which is also moving at ten to thirty-five knots. Wind, real and apparent; temperature; course and speed of the enemy; course and speed of your own ship must all be taken into consideration and allowed for if hits are to be made.

TORPEDOES

TORPEDOES are used in our Navy by submarines, destroyers, planes, and motor torpedo boats. Some of our oldest cruisers are still equipped with torpedo tubes, but in general the modern tendency in our Fleet is to make the cruiser a gun platform unencumbered by torpedoes. The torpedo, like the mine, is often the weapon of the inferior naval power, but great results can be achieved with it, if it is properly used, by any fleet.

Torpedoes are expensive instruments of destruction, costing, in this country from $6,000 to $15,000 each. They have one great advantage over the shell; they travel underwater, and hence can attack the weakest portion of an enemy ship, the underwater hull, which is usually of triple thickness, but which is not built of the great slabs of armor that protect the water line and sides and decks. No practical way of armoring a ship's underwater hull has yet been found; the resultant weight is far too great. Protection is, therefore, achieved by building the ship often with triple thicknesses of plating, so-called double, or triple bottoms, and by subdividing the interior into many different water-tight compartments to localize damage.

Torpedoes are sleek, shining cylinders of steel—all of the modern ones in our Navy 21-inches in diameter (there are a few 18-inchers in our motor torpedo boats) —which consist essentially of two main sections, the pro-

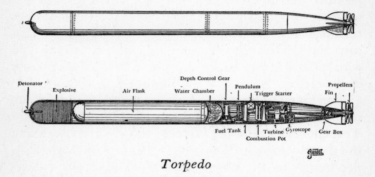

Torpedo

pelling part and the explosive part or warhead, which is fitted with a primer and up to 600 pounds of T.N.T. Torpedoes are fired from torpedo tubes—or hollow cylinders of metal—either by a charge of black powder or by compressed air. As they are ejected from the tubes, a starting lever is tripped which actuates the torpedo's propelling mechanism, and once the torpedo is in the water, it moves under its own power.

Propulsive power in our Navy is furnished by a mixture of compressed air, alcohol (which the sailors call "pink lady"), and water. The compressed air is contained in an air flask in the torpedo at several hundred pounds' pressure, and the torpedo is charged with it before it is fired. When the starting mechanism is actuated on firing, the compressed air hisses through little pipe lines into a combustion pot and mixes there with a jet of alcohol and water. The alcohol is ignited by a special ignition system; the burning mixture is transformed in the combustion pot into a form of steam and gas under pressure and is piped to two little rotating turbines, where it impinges on the steel blades and turns over the turbines. The turbines drive the propeller shafts which turn one inside the other in opposite directions and which drive two propellers, also turning in opposite directions.

Horizontal and vertical rudders control the direction of the torpedo and keep it on an even horizontal plane. Torpedoes can be set to travel at any desired depth and the depth-setting is made before the torpedo is fired, depending upon the target. Against a target like a deep-draft battleship, for instance, the torpedo might be set to travel at twenty to twenty-three feet beneath the surface; against a destroyer, five to ten feet would be the depth-setting.

Little gyroscopes which are spun and kept spinning by a jet of compressed air control the rudders and keep the torpedo on the desired course at the desired depth. Sometimes, from the shock of firing, they "tumble" and the torpedo goes wild, perhaps leaping out of the water like a flying fish, or turning viciously in circles. In target practice when torpedoes are fitted with dummy practice heads, it is not unusual for torpedoes to circle about and hit the ship that has fired them.

Torpedoes are difficult to control, and if seen in time,

ships can maneuver to avoid them, so that they achieve greatest results when fired in "spreads" at relatively close distances. They have speeds varying from 25 to 50 knots and may travel through the water from 6,000 to 30,000 yards.

MINES

MINES are spheres (or torpedo-shaped objects) of metal encasing charges of T.N.T. varying in size (depending on the size of the mine) from about 250 to 650 pounds of explosive.

There are various types of mines; the most usual is the anchored mine, held to the bottom by a steel anchor (which is also the little carriage on which it rides and is launched from the ship that lays it) and equipped with "horns" or contact points on its spherical surface which cause the mine to explode when these points are touched by a ship.

These are known as contact mines and can be laid in depths up to about 600 feet. They can be set to float (before they are laid) at nearly any desired depth beneath the surface, so that they will be touched by the bottom of a surface ship or by a submarine beneath the surface. The famous North Sea mine barrage, laid in the closing days of the World War chiefly by American effort, was intended primarily to bottle up the German submarines.

Free or floating mines are against international law

and are not supposed to be used ordinarily, but sometimes are. Often anchored mines break away from their
moorings during storms and become free mines dangerous to friend and foe alike.

The newest type of mine—one which was tried during

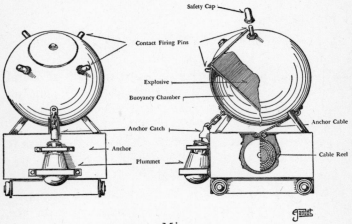

Mine

the World War, but with unsatisfactory results—is the
magnetic mine which the Germans have used with such
success in this war. It is laid by submarines or planes or
surface vessels; sinks to the bottom of shallow water
(usually not much more than 40 feet, in less depth if
possible) and remains there until a steel-hulled vessel
passes over it or near enough to it to actuate its mag-
netic-electrical mechanism. Then the mine, contrary to
the popular assumption, does *not* leap up from its sea
bed, as the Sunday supplement writers would have us

believe and rush like a leech to the bottom of the passing ship. (One type has been tried, however, which floats to the surface when a ship passes.) But it does explode where it is, in its bed of mud on the sea floor, and the explosion is caused by the ship's passage nearby. The magnetic field of the ship actuates tiny electrical instruments in the mine (usually a magnetic needle), the electrical current induced in these instruments is "boosted" by a battery and moves a needle or in other ways sets off a primer which in turn explodes the main explosive charge. The concussive effect of this explosion transmitted through the water strains or breaks the passing ship's hull and sinks or damages her severely or lightly, depending on the strength of the ship and her distance from the mine.

Minesweepers, equipped with wire sweeps, are useful against the ordinary contact anchored mine. The sweeps cut the mine cable; it bobs to the surface and is exploded by gunfire from a safe distance. Men-of-war protect themselves against anchored mines by utilizing paravanes, or torpedo-shaped objects trailed from the bow of the ship underwater at about a 45-degree angle with the bow. Anchored mines rarely if ever hit the bow of a ship, for the bow wave throws the anchored mine off to one side, and the tendency of the mine swaying on its cable is then to swing back and hit the side of the ship, usually at about a quarter of its length from its bow or amidships. Paravanes, held by wire cables to the underwater foot of the vessel, are equipped with cutting jaws; the mine cable slides down the sweep wire to these cutters, is cut, and the mine bobs to the surface.

Against magnetic mines a new form of protection has been devised, and consists of a nest of electric cables usually around the outside of a ship near its upper deck. These cables can be supplied with electricity from the ship's generators and serve to "de-magnetize" the ship or to reverse its magnetic field, thus neutralizing the apparatus of the magnetic mine. This is known as "degaussing apparatus" and our naval vessels are being equipped with it.

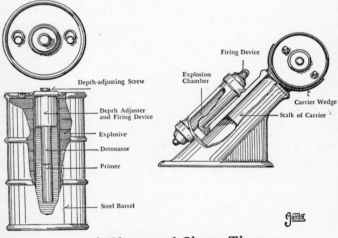

Depth Adjusting Screw

Depth Adjuster and Firing Device

Explosive

Detonator

Primer

Steel Barrel

Firing Device

Explosion Chamber

Carrier Wedge

Stalk of Carrier

Depth Charge and Charge Thrower

DEPTH CHARGES

THE depth charge procures its destructive effect by transmitting the concussive blow of the explosion of T.N.T. underwater through the water. A depth charge is not a missile designed to hit a submarine or to explode on contact; it has much the same effect as the magnetic mine.

It is a cylinder of thin metal filled with T.N.T. (usually about 300 pounds) and with a hydrostatic firing mechanism, which can be set for any desired depth. The depth charge is rolled over the stern of a speeding surface ship, or thrown out from the sides by Y guns (so-called because of their shape). The charges are dropped —sometimes in a diamond-shaped pattern—sometimes in a spiral pattern, to cover a great surface of sea around an area where a submerged submarine is thought to be. The location of the submarine can often be plotted by taking bearings with the aid of a ship's underwater listening, and submarine detecting apparatus.

COMMUNICATIONS

COMMUNICATIONS in the Navy are of almost co-equal importance with gunnery and engineering. If one ship cannot transmit accurately and rapidly to another in the heat of battle the battle may be lost. Jutland, the great battle between the British and German Fleets during the World War, provides a graphic example of this: Admiral Beatty, scouting for the enemy, made contact with the Germans, but many of his reports to Admiral Jellicoe never got through and the latter was materially handicapped in his decisions.

The Navy uses many different systems of communications and usually parallels one with the other when possible, so that a message is certain to get through.

There are, of course, two main communication subdivisions—internal communications, or the communications from one part of a ship to another; and the external communications. The latter is by far the more important, since messengers can, if absolutely essential, bridge a disruption of communications aboard ship, but information must be transmitted from one ship to another or from ship to shore or plane by radio, sound, or visual methods.

In internal communications the telephone is used, both an ordinary ship's dial telephone like that ashore, and the so-called battle circuits, manned during general quarters or drills or maneuverings. Visual electrically operated indicators and recorders—from the bridge to the engine room, etc. (such as "⅓ speed; Full Speed," etc.), are also used, and voice tubes, which now have chemical filters to prevent gas from penetrating the interior of the ship, are other means of communication.

For external communications the most important method by far is radio; indeed radio has changed naval war.

RADIO

EVERY ship in the Navy, except small boats, is equipped with radio transmitting and receiving apparatus, most of it extremely powerful and capable of sending and receiving at great distances. Most ships are also equipped with radio telephones, which are used over short distances. Code used is the ordinary international Morse, but any important message is coded by means of a coding machine or book; that is, another letter or figure is substituted for the original letter or figure. The "key" to these codes is changed frequently; the codes and keys and coding boxes are carefully locked in safes and are among the most secret of the Navy's possessions. Code books and signal books are equipped with lead backs, and they are to be burned or thrown overboard in case of imminent capture or loss of the ship to an enemy to prevent the codes from falling into enemy hands.

VISUAL

VISUAL methods of communication include flag hoists, semaphore and flashing light.

Signal flags hoisted to the signal yardarms of ships are, to the average spectator, colorful bunting; to the initiated navy man every hoist means something which will be found, if he doesn't know the meaning by heart, in the signal book. The flags are international signal flags, differently marked in blue, yellow, red, and white, with each flag standing for a specific letter of the alphabet.

Some special naval pennants indicate numerals and other specific naval designations. Navy men call the blue and white burgee flag which stands for A "Affirmative," so that when the signal is read and written down, the recorder will not make any mistakes and think he has heard Z instead of A. B is Baker; C is Cast, and so on. Strings of these flags, hoisted to the yardarm in a certain order, mean different things; the combinations are endless.

Another means of visual signaling is by semaphore flags—two hand flags held by a signalman. The position in which he holds these flags designates the letter he is forming, and by holding them in different positions he spells out words rapidly.

Blinkers, searchlights, or other forms of flashing light usually employ the dot-and-dash method of the radio.

SOUND

SOUND signaling is the least important of the methods of naval communication, though supersonic or beyond audible sound waves may have increasing importance. Underwater sound oscillators are used by submarines and some other vessels.

Whistle signals are important in the sea-going rules of the road and in maneuvering. One long blast means, "I am directing my course to starboard"; two long blasts indicate the signaling ship is directing its course to port. Long blasts are also blown on the whistle at intervals when the ship is underway in a fog; at anchor the ship's bell is rung rapidly during fog.

Megaphoned directions by voice are often used when a vessel is coming alongside a dock, and occasionally when maneuvering with small vessels, such as motor torpedo boats.

CHAPTER SEVEN

BASES

BASES are just as important an element of Sea Power as are ships. For, as Captain Hopwood's *Laws of the Navy* points out:

> "When the ship that is tired returneth,
>   With the signs of the sea showing plain,
> Men place her in dock for a season,
>   And her speed she reneweth again."

Sea Power cannot operate without a great and vast complex of shore establishments, ranging from drydocks and shipbuilding ways to ammunition depots and ordnance plants.

The Navy's shore establishments are of many different types; to facilitate their administration the nation has been divided into naval districts, each commanded by a commandant with the rank of rear admiral.

Headquarters of these districts are as shown below; each of these districts includes that portion of the nation adjacent to these headquarters.

DISTRICT	HEADQUARTERS
First	Boston, Massachusetts
Second	(Included in First)

DISTRICT	HEADQUARTERS
Third	New York, New York
Fourth	Philadelphia, Pennsylvania
Fifth	Norfolk, Virginia
Sixth, Seventh	Charleston, South Carolina
Eighth	New Orleans, Louisiana
Ninth	Great Lakes, Illinois
Tenth	San Juan, Puerto Rico (includes all Caribbean islands)
Eleventh	San Diego, California
Twelfth	San Francisco, California
Thirteenth	Seattle, Washington
Fourteenth	Pearl Harbor, Hawaii (includes Pacific islands, except Guam and Samoa)
Fifteenth	Canal Zone (Balboa)
Sixteenth	Cavite, Philippines
Naval Station	Alaska (at present floating headquarters only)
Naval Station	Guam
Naval Station	American Samoa (Tutuila)

Naval districts are territorial divisions, and the naval shore activities within those districts are supervised by the commandant of the district concerned.

Nearly every naval district has as the most important and largest of its activities a navy yard for construction, and/or repair of ships, with drydocks, shipbuilding ways, machine shops, and other facilities. These yards are not primarily operating bases, or anchorages, or fuel depots, although ships can find wharfage and oil facilities at each yard. They are primarily repair, overhaul, and construction yards, and each yard has some particular specialty in addition to its general shipbuilding and ship repair facilities. For instance the Portsmouth Navy Yard (New Hampshire) is limited largely to the construction and repair of submarines and small surface craft and it builds electrical appliances for naval vessels, while the Boston yard, in addition to its ship construction and up-keep facilities, is specially charged with the manufacture of anchor chain and cordage for naval vessels, while Portsmouth, Va. (or Norfolk), makes metal ship furniture. The Navy Yards are:

Portsmouth, New Hampshire
Boston, Massachusetts
New York, New York
Philadelphia, Pennsylvania
Washington, D. C. (repairs a few small naval vessels, but chiefly important as site of Naval Gun Factory which makes most of naval guns and much other ordnance equipment)
Portsmouth (or Norfolk), Virginia
Charleston, South Carolina
Mare Island (San Francisco), California
Puget Sound, or Bremerton, Washington
Pearl Harbor, Territory of Hawaii
Cavite, Philippine Islands

These yards are run and administered by naval officers—some of them line officers, and a considerable number of them specialists of the staff corps. A great number of civilian employees, who are constantly increasing

during the present emergency, staff the navy yards, and
every kind of trade and profession from draftsman and
accountant to shipfitter is to be found on the civil
service rolls.

Naval operating bases are bases equipped with drydocks and supply and repair facilities, which are not
ship construction bases, but are intended primarily to
service the operating ships of the Fleet. Wharfage and
supplies of fuel and stores and ammunition are essential to this end. There are now four principal bases of
this character, at Norfolk, Virginia; San Diego, California; San Francisco; and Balboa, Canal Zone. Others,
not yet dignified by the name, really exist at Pearl
Harbor (with an outlying anchorage at Lahaina Roads);
New York; Newport; San Pedro; Puget Sound; Cavite,
Philippine Islands; and San Juan. Ships of the sky and
of the sea can operate from all these places, and though
facilities in some of them are not adequate for a complete fleet, yet all of them can support a considerable
number of ships. San Juan and Cavite and Newport
are particularly limited by inadequate, or total lack
of, drydocks, though San Juan's need is being filled.

Naval stations of various types, kinds, and sizes, ranging from protected anchorages to fortified harbors where
fuel is available are scattered all over the United States
and at outlying points in both Atlantic and Pacific.

These stations have been considerably augmented in
recent years by development of Pacific islands—a development which is still incomplete—and by the acquisition
of a good many island sites from Britain in the Atlantic-
Caribbean area. Naval stations are at Newport, Rhode

Island (torpedo station); New London, Connecticut (submarine base); Quantico, Virginia, Parris Island, South Carolina, and San Diego, California (marine barracks); and Key West, Florida; Guantanamo Bay, Cuba (fleet anchorage and fueling station); St. Thomas, Virgin Islands; New Orleans, Louisiana. Outlying bases acquired as the result of the Anglo-American destroyer-naval base-deal are sites at: Newfoundland; Bermuda; Bahamas; Jamaica; Antigua; St. Lucia; Trinidad; and British Guiana.

Trinidad will be a principal fleet operating base, when facilities there are completed, perhaps two or more years from now, and will serve as a base from which our Fleet can operate to protect the northeastern part of South America. Most of the other points will be submarine bases, bases for light vessels or naval air stations.

At Panama, a naval air station and submarine base is already established (and has been enlarged recently) on the Atlantic side, in addition to the operating base on the Pacific side.

In the Pacific, there are naval stations, air or surface, at Sitka, Alaska, and others under construction at Kodiak, Aleutians; and Dutch Harbor, Unalaska. A ring of small, outlying bases is being flung outward from Hawaii, mostly for air use, but some of them also serviceable to submarines and small craft. These include Midway, Wake, Johnston, Palmyra, Rose, and Canton Islands.

In the Philippines, Olongapo is a naval station (in addition to the yard at Cavite), but has been inoperative.

In addition to all these activities, there are naval air stations for either land or sea planes or both at or near practically all of the surface bases mentioned, and a good many others beside. Jacksonville, Miami, and Pensacola, Florida, and Corpus Christi, Texas, are the centers of the Navy's air training program. There are Naval Reserve air bases scattered throughout the country, and there are important naval air stations, in addition to those already listed, at Alameda, California; Tongue Point, Oregon; and Kaneohe Bay, Territory Hawaii.

And finally, there are a great number of naval ordnance facilities, ammunition and mine depots, ordnance plants, and torpedo stations. (The Navy has three of the latter: Newport, Rhode Island; Alexandria, Virginia; and Keyport, Washington; the latter an upkeep and overhaul station only, not manufacturing.)

There is a naval research laboratory in Anacostia, D. C., and an engineering experiment station in Annapolis, in addition to scores of other less important naval activities. For a sea-going organization must, if it is to be a real blue-water "outfit," keep its feet firmly planted on the land.

The most important requisite for a good base is that it must be *secure;* that is, ships must be able to lie in it for repairs or overhaul safe from the assaults of the enemy. This means, in this modern day, that bases too close to enemy, or potential enemy possessions, may be too exposed to permit a fleet to be based upon them with safety; the island of England now constantly exposed to air attack is the best example of this.

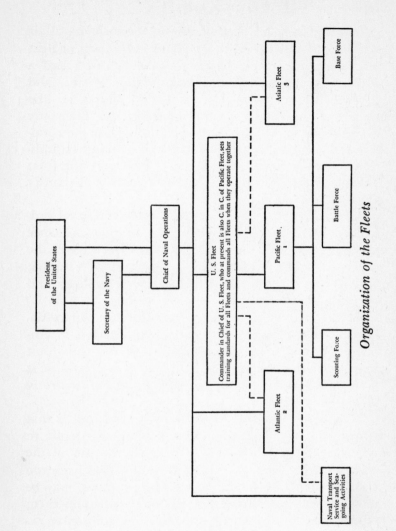

President
of the United States

Secretary of the Navy

Chief of Naval Operations

U. S. Fleet

Commander in Chief of U. S. Fleet, who at present is also C. in C. of Pacific Fleet, sets
training standards for all Fleets and commands all Fleets when they operate together

Atlantic Fleet
2

Pacific Fleet
1

Asiatic Fleet
3

Naval Transport
Service and Sea-
going Activities

Scouting Force

Battle Force

Base Force

Organization of the Fleets

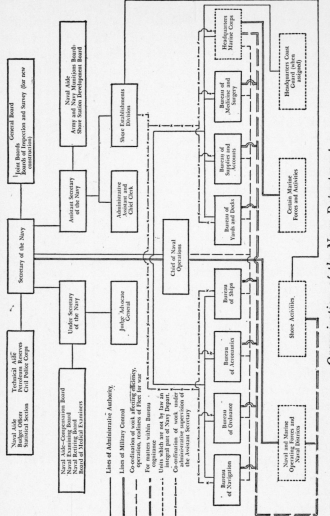

Organization of the Navy Department

A base must also, of course, have a favorable geographical location so as to permit the fleet to best maneuver in the waters it wishes to dominate. Bases must also have resources; the best base for this reason is a continental base with the resources of a continent tied to it by railroad lines and roads. And of course bases must be protected, with submarine nets and mines, with coast defense guns (usually manned by the Army; in the case of a few outlying advanced bases that might be seized in war, by the Marines) with antiaircraft guns and defending planes, with small forces of submarine chasers, etc. And they must have equipment and resources—fuel oil tanks, preferably underground; tugs; small craft; cranes; machine shops; wharfs and drydocks; etc.

Each shore establishment of the United States Navy has a commanding officer, who in turn may receive orders from the commandant of the naval district in which his station is situated and/or from the Navy Department.

The Navy Department is the head of this vast hierarchy of rank and complex of industry; the Navy Department is in charge of both shore and sea-going establishments, but it is dedicated to the principle that the shore establishments exist to serve the Fleet, that the tail must not wag the dog.

The accompanying chart shows the shore organization of the Navy, and it is not necessary to elaborate the details greatly. The President is commander in chief of the Navy, and the secretary of the Navy, a civilian, who now has a civilian undersecretary and assistant

secretary as his assistants, heads the Navy Department.
The senior ranking officer of the entire Navy is the chief
of naval operations, who holds the rank of full admiral
during his tour of duty (usually four years). The assistant secretary of the Navy is especially charged with
the Navy Yards and shore establishments; the chief of
naval operations is more concerned, as his title implies,
with actual fleet operations, with plans and with what
the Fleet needs. Nevertheless the district commandants
come under the chief of naval operations in the chain
of command, just as the commander in chief of the
Fleets do

The Navy Department is broken down into a number of bureaus and offices and Congress appropriates
funds directly to these subdivisions, rather than to the
Navy Department as a whole. There are nine principal
divisions: the Bureau of Navigation (which oddly
enough has charge of naval personnel in addition to
charts, hydrographic surveys, etc.); Bureau of Ordnance
(in charge of ordnance equipment); Bureau of Ships
(ship-construction, including engineering); Bureau of
Aeronautics; Bureau of Yards and Docks; Bureau of
Supplies and Accounts; Bureau of Medicine and Sur-
gery; Major-General Commandant of the Marine Corps
and Judge-Advocate General of the Navy.

The Bureau of Yards and Docks has cognizance over
most of the principal navy yards and some other shore
establishments, with the Bureau of Aeronautics directly
interested in the naval air fields. The Shore Establishments Division, under the assistant secretary of the
Navy, is also concerned with the Navy's land activities.

Local district commandants are responsible in time of war for the local naval defenses of the harbors in their area and of the coast (in cooperation, of course, with the Army). For instance a submarine net to be stretched across the Narrows, entrance to New York Harbor, has been manufactured and is ready at the New York Navy Yard and that net will be tended from a base at Staten Island, New York. Minesweepers, in case of war, will operate from that base, out past Ambrose Lightship, and along the focus of shipping lanes that lead into the harbor. There will also be motor torpedo boats, patrol craft, sub-chasers and some planes from naval fields in the district—all for local defense and patrol work, under the direction of the commandant, Third Naval District, with headquarters in Manhattan, New York City.

CHAPTER EIGHT

THE FLEET

THE United States Fleet is probably the most homogeneous fighting unit upon the seas. To see it operate at advanced battle practice, its disparate units marching and counter-marching in ordered ranks across the tumbling surface of the sea; to watch it, powerful and mighty, surge in the nice articulation of its strength against an imaginary enemy is to observe the unbelievable. And to see it, its guns thundering, the white wakes of its torpedoes lacing the surface, the drone of its planes filling the skies, is to watch the ordered chaos of Armageddon. For a well-handled and homogeneous fleet, in maneuvers or battle, presents an amazing example of flexible strength; the ships and planes and men move on unheard order as if some giant and omnipotent hand hidden in the clouds were pulling them, like puppets, upon strings.

The United States Fleet, as of February 1, 1941, was re-constituted into three Fleets, comprising, except for local district craft and the Naval Transportation Service, all our ships afloat. The United States Fleet, with one officer with the rank of admiral designated as commander in chief, is now subdivided into the Pacific Fleet, the Atlantic Fleet (almost equal in size, though scarcely in fleet combat efficiency), and the Asiatic Fleet.

The Atlantic Fleet today is composed largely of special task forces, but it is organized along the same general lines as the Pacific Fleet and is readily expansible as new ships become available. The Asiatic Fleet is only a covering or delaying force of three light cruisers, and a few submarines and destroyers and naval patrol planes, a Fleet which could threaten to inflict severe losses on any enemy but which could not defeat him.

Approximately 50 per cent of the fighting strength of our Navy is concentrated in the Pacific Fleet, which, since the European War began, has been based in and around the Hawaiian Islands.

This Fleet consists of battleships, aircraft carriers, and cruisers, destroyers, submarines, minecraft, patrol planes, and auxiliaries of all types. A portion of the Fleet Marine Force, an expeditionary force of the Marines organized for instant active duty, is also attached to it and frequently operates with it.

The Pacific Fleet is divided into three principal forces—the Battle Force, the Scouting Force, and the Base Force—and each of these is subdivided into types, and these in turn into divisions or squadrons.

The Battle Force, commanded by a vice admiral, is what its name implies; it consists of the main combatant units of the Fleet—all its battle-line strength of battleships; the light cruisers; the aircraft carriers; the destroyers and the minecraft. The Scouting Force, charged with the duties of scouting for the enemy and developing his dispositions, includes heavy cruisers and submarines and patrol planes. The Base Force consists of the auxiliary, supply, and repair vessels and tenders, and mobile target units, as well as planes of the utility wing which help to service the Fleet.

Each of these main forces is commanded by a vice, or rear, admiral and each of these is subdivided into tactical units. The battleships are subdivided into three divisions—Battleship Divisions 1, 2, and 4—each of three ships, each commanded by a rear admiral. The cruisers are also divided into divisions, each of four ships each. The destroyers are divided into divisions, squadrons, and flotillas with four destroyers to a division, two divisions (eight ships) plus a leader to each squadron, and four squadrons (thirty-six ships) to a flotilla. There are two flotillas, each with a light cruiser as flagship, in the Battle Force. The minelayers are organized— four light ones to a division—and the minesweepers, four to a division. The Base Force is organized more loosely, since it is composed of different types of ships of different sizes and since it is not called upon for the careful tactical maneuvering of the combatant types.

The patrol planes are organized in squadrons of twelve each and in wings of three to five squadrons (plus sometimes a utility unit) in each wing.

The Pacific Fleet is the most fully-organized and complete fleet, but the other two are organized in embryo along the same general lines as the Pacific Fleet with necessary alterations in the organization due to the different number of ships and different types available. There are no main task *forces,* for instance, in the

Asiatic Fleet, although they may be organized when sufficient new ships are on hand. The Atlantic Fleet, which has been greatly reinforced in the past year by new vessels and by ships shifted from the Pacific, is now composed of a strong force of battleships, supported by all other types.

Our Fleets are organized for greatest combat efficiency, but as new lessons of war are learned and new and improved types of vessels become available, organizations naturally must change. At present, in the midst of war and tremendous expansion, the tactical structure of the Fleet is subject to intermittent change, for navies like armies are in a period of tactical flux.

The three main components of any fleet, however, are likely to remain constant, and it is these three components that are represented in our full-grown Pacific Fleet by the Battle Force, the Scouting Force, and the Base Force. The Battle Force and the Scouting Force are the fighting components of the Fleet; the Base Force is composed of the auxiliaries, plodding and vulnerable, but absolutely essential, which service the Fleet—the oilers, repair and supply ships, tugs, etc. They take their name from the fact that they do most of their work in base; they are not designed for combat (although they mount a few small guns for some protection) and would never take part in a fleet action. But they are mobile and can accompany the Fleet and can make available their facilities at some outlying advanced island base which the Fleet may seize.

The Battle Force packs the knock-out right-hand

punch of the Navy; it is comprised of the battle line and the destroyers ready to deliver their torpedo attacks against the enemy battle line, and the light cruisers prepared to support such a destroyer attack, to repel similar enemy destroyer attacks, and to screen the battleships. It consists, too, of the Fleet's ship-based planes—the catapulted planes from the battleships and cruisers, mainly for spotting and scouting work—and the combat planes from the carriers.

The Scouting Force conducts blue-water reconnaissance and searches out the enemy. The submarines are the long-distance scouts and because of their ability to conceal themselves can make their way close to some enemy port or near to some bottleneck of shipping lanes, like the Strait of Tsushima, and there lie to spy upon, and report upon, enemy ship movements. The long-range patrol planes, flying day after day on ceaseless patrol of great segments of ocean, can spot any enemy forces and, similarly, are able by radio to report their whereabouts, course, and disposition to the commander of the Scouting Force who then passes on the reports to the commander in chief. And the heavy cruisers can develop these early contacts, and with the bruising power of their eight-inch guns, can push through the enemy's outer screen and determine his strength and dispositions. Cruisers are able to operate in weather conditions which may hopelessly handicap the operations of planes, and perhaps submarines.

The Scouting Force in a fleet engagement or in cruising formations also acts as a screen for the heavier ships;

these screens of light forces prevent the enemy from developing contact and from determining our own strength and dispositions.

There is one other element of the Fleet which deserves special mention here. And that is the Fleet Marine Force, a special mobile expeditionary force of U. S. Marines, which comes under the direct command of the commander in chief, U. S. Fleet. Half of this force is normally stationed at Quantico, Virginia, half at San Diego, California, but it is frequently transported to the Caribbean area on the East Coast or to San Clemente, off the California Coast, or to the Hawaiian Islands area for training.

It is an amphibian force, and, together with army units, it is being organized as a quick-moving striking group. The Force is being organized in two divisions—the standard combat organization of land troops—each of which will number about 11,000 men. They will be the first divisions in the world to include under one divisional command, tanks, planes, parachute troops, reconnaissance elements, antitank and antiaircraft weapons, and field artillery and infantry. One parachute battalion of 400 men, the nucleus of which is now being trained at the Naval Air Station at Lakehurst, N. J., will eventually be assigned to each division. Each division will also have seventy-two of the Army's $12\frac{1}{2}$-ton light tanks, and 120 planes—bombers, scouts, and fighters.

All this and a great deal more equipment is designed to be loaded aboard transports at a moment's notice

and the "gyrenes" or "leathernecks" are ready for a
frolic or a fray in any part of the world. The marines
have developed special landing equipment, among it
the so-called "alligator" (with which the Army is also
being supplied). This is a flat-bottomed steel landing
boat which in its experimental form has climbed a 55-
degree slope, swum through the sea at 10 miles an hour
and across land at 25, knocked down eight or ten-inch
trees, and carried a load of 7,000 pounds. The boat is
in effect a sort of ocean-going tank, without the tank's
thick armor (though the new models will have some
armor and some guns). It has caterpillar-paddle-wheel
treads; that is, fin-like extensions from the continuous
tracks which run underneath the hull of the boat, give
it propulsive power when the contraption is in the
water and act as cleats in mud, sand, or on land. These
boats can be carried on transports, loaded with marines
and their equipment, and lowered, fully loaded, by
crane from the transports' decks into the sea. Then,
under their own power, they can "swim" to shore,
waddle across coral ledges, climb up a sandy beach, and
push into a forest until the marines, hidden from
"enemy fire," can safely disembark.

The two marine divisions, which form our Fleet
Marine Force are intended for operations with the
Fleet; the marines are amphibious soldiers, and these
divisions might be utilized to seize some advanced base,
or to force a landing and establish a beach-head on
some hostile shore to be held until the Army could get
there.

The modern Marine Corps also has devised another

interesting type of organization, the "Defense Battalion." Each of the six battalions now organized is to be armed with antiaircraft and coast defense guns, machine guns, and infantry weapons, and is trained to accompany the Fleet, and to organize and defend some outlying island base that might be seized by the Fleet after war started.

The modern marines are therefore not only "semper fidelis" ("always faithful") as their motto states, but they must be always ready for high-seas duty with the Fleet.

CHAPTER NINE

HOW THE FLEET IS USED

NAVIES can be used either in wars of assault or wars of
attrition; they are capable either of fighting fleet ac-
tions or of conducting the long, slow processes of the
blockade.

The use of the fleet is determined by the grand
strategy of the war; but the dispositions of the fleet in
battle are determined by the *tactical* plans of the commander in chief. *Strategy* concerns the broad-scale utili-
zation of a navy in a theater of war; *tactics,* the handling
of a fleet or a ship in the presence of the enemy.

The objective of a fleet, as we have seen, is to insure
the safety of sea communications for its own country,
and to deny like security to an enemy. No fleet or fleets
are, or can be, strong enough to make all the sea lanes
of the world secure; the essential task of a fleet, therefore, is to safeguard the sea lanes which are vital or
highly important to the country whose flag it flies.

If this can be done by destroying the enemy fleet, so
much the better. Commanders in chief of great fleets
always hope that the enemy fleet may accept the gauge
of battle, and thereby control of the sea may be largely
determined. But such great sea battles are, in modern
naval war, the exception, not the rule. For few Sea Powers are of even approximately equal strength; the in-

ferior Sea Power may well refuse to accept the risk of
battle and may elect to wage a war of attrition against
a superior enemy. This is the kind of war that Germany
has been waging on the seas against Britain; it is the
kind of war that Germany waged in the World War.

Today that type of warfare is immeasurably helped
by the plane and the submarine. No Sea Power can call
itself queen of the seas unless it can also master the
air and the submarine threat to the commerce lanes
that are essential to it.

The two main ways in which Sea Power can be employed have been well illustrated by the European
War. In the Mediterranean the British Fleet has been
utilized more or less as a fleet unit in operations against
the Italian Fleet and in aiding the British armies. In
the Atlantic the British Fleet's chief duties (in addition
to keeping in check the surface navy of Germany) have
been to guard merchant shipping and patrol the seas
in attempts to ward off the attrition attacks which Germany has been making by submarine and plane.

One type of warfare is very different from the other.

Co-ordinated fleet operations culminating in a great
naval battle require precise training and exact gunnery
and seamanship. The battle may be to the strong, but
it is also to the well trained.

Attrition warfare, or defense against it, also requires
careful training, but it requires, too, a great number of
armed merchant vessels, a great number of escort vessels, destroyers, submarine chasers, cruisers, etc., and a
thorough patience, dogged courage, and eternal vig-
ilance.

A fleet, operating as a unit, uses different tactics, different maneuvering formations, and different cruising formations, depending upon the situation of the moment, depending also upon the number of men-of-war and train (supply and repair ships) on hand, and their characteristics. The maneuvering formations, cruising, and battle dispositions shown in the accompanying pages are not to be taken as completely faithful to the actuality; these formations and dispositions are modified and revised from year to year, and the United States Navy keeps them carefully secret. But the sketches do approximate formations that have been used and typify the manner in which the Fleet is disposed in wartime.

Ordinarily, both in cruising and in battle, ships steam in column. Battleships steam one behind the other, interval about 500 yards, destroyers about 250 yards apart. At times the column may be staggered or open, with the second ship off to the port quarter of the first, the third directly behind the first, about 1,000 yards astern, the fourth behind the second, etc.

When ships are in column a simultaneous 90-degree turn will bring them into line abreast; a 180-degree turn will reverse their direction. The Fleet constantly practices these turns, and although they seem simple, it is difficult when a great many ships are involved, to keep positions accurately.

Cruising formations for the Fleet are designed to give the maximum of security and at the same time to permit the most rapid possible deployment into battle formations. Cruising formations are simple enough if only combatant ships are with the Fleet, but if trans-

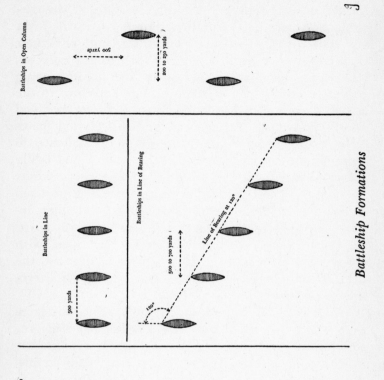

Battleships in Column

500 yards

Battleships in Line

500 yards

Battleships in Open Column

500 yards

200 to 250 yards

Battleships in Line of Bearing

500 to 700 yards

120°

Line of Bearing at 120°

Battleship Formations

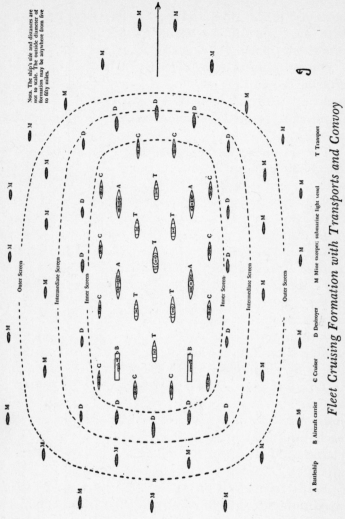

Note. The ship's size and distances are not to scale. The outside diameter of formation may be anywhere from five to fifty miles.

Outer Screen

Intermediate Screen

Inner Screen

Inner Screen

Intermediate Screen

Outer Screen

A Battleship   B Aircraft carrier   C Cruiser   D Destroyer   M Mine sweeper; submarine light vessel   T Transport

Fleet Cruising Formation with Transports and Convoy

ports and supply ships and the Fleet's train (auxiliaries), with the Fleet Marine Force, for instance, have to be protected, then the problem is more difficult.

One solution that has been tested has been a circular cruising formation with the vulnerable transports and noncombatant vessels at the center of a wide circle of ships, which spread out in concentric circles over miles of ocean.

The transports, in irregular formation and zigzagging, are closely convoyed by a number of destroyers, usually with a column of battleships on either flank, and perhaps a light cruiser ahead and astern. The aircraft carriers, also escorted by antisubmarine craft, may be directly astern. Flung around this center core are successive circles of lighter vessels: first heavy cruisers; then a circle of light cruisers; then destroyers; and finally on the outermost rim a circle of submarines, minelayers, minesweepers, and small craft. Scouting far ahead will be other submarines, and possibly all or part of the Scouting Force, while long-range patrol planes and planes from the carriers will maintain a continuous sweep back and forth above the ocean.

This sort of cruising formation gives good protection against submarine attack, since an enemy submarine must penetrate successive rings or screens of light craft, each equipped with listening apparatus and depth charges. But it is not so well suited to resist heavy air attack.

Battle formations are all so arranged as to bring the maximum strength of the battle line into action. The entire disposition of the Fleet in battle depends upon

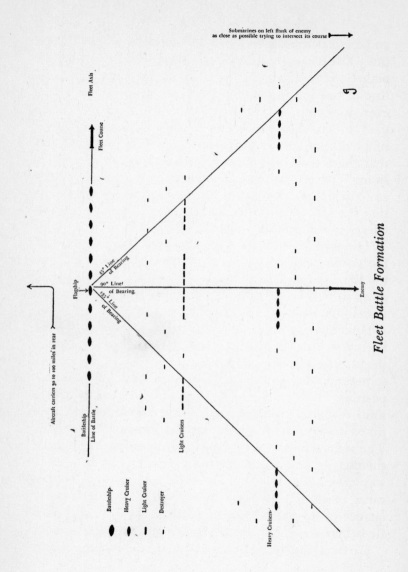

Fleet Battle Formation

Submarines on left flank of enemy as close as possible trying to intersect its course →

Fleet Axis

Fleet Course

15° Line of Bearing

90° Line of Bearing

135° Line of Bearing

Flagship

Aircraft carriers 90 to 100 miles in rear

Battleship Line of Battle

Light Cruisers

Heavy Cruisers

Enemy

Battleship

Heavy Cruiser

Light Cruiser

Destroyer

and pivots around the great battleships of the battle
line. These usually steam in column, which is a flexible
maneuvering formation from which they can shift into
line of bearing (see sketch), or line. The column, however, is not now so rigid and precise a thing as it once
used to be; it is usually open column, and the divisions of battleships maneuver semi-independently so
that there may be considerable intervals between divisions. The battleships are maneuvered in such a way
as to try to keep the enemy approximately abeam so
that the full weight of the ships' main batteries may be
effectively employed.

The aircraft carriers must stay out of gun range of
the enemy, and they are usually well out of sight over
the horizon, perhaps thirty to sixty miles, or even more,
away from the battleships. They are screened by a few
destroyers and perhaps cruisers.

Heavy cruisers may take position in the van or rear of
the battle line—probably in the van and on the battleships' engaged bow—and light cruisers and destroyers
sometime during the course of the action will take
position between the battle line and the enemy battle
line, ready to repel enemy destroyer attacks and prepared to launch destroyer attacks against the enemy.
The submarines, if they can get into position, may place
themselves well ahead off the enemy's bow, in such a
way that his course will intersect with theirs, but because of their slow underwater speed they will get a
chance to fire their torpedoes only if the course of battle brings the enemy fleet down upon their position.

Carriers and heavy cruisers (or battle cruisers, when

and if we construct any) can also be used as a detached
striking group, their objective the enemy carriers or
detached forces of the enemy. Such a group, using its
high speed, might swing around the stern or bow of the
enemy, and fall upon the enemy carriers in the rear or
perhaps strike the enemy's bow or unengaged flank.

In actual battle, skill in maneuvering plays a large
premium, but luck is always a partial arbiter. If a commander can catch the enemy ships silhouetted against
a rising or setting sun, while his own ships are in dark-
ness he has a tremendous initial advantage. In maneuvering he must avoid, at all costs, placing his ships in
such a position that his vessels are "enfiladed"; that is,
placed one behind the other in relation to the enemy,
so that "shorts" or "overs" from enemy salvos are bound
to hit something.

A maneuver that has been tried with success in past
battles—notably at the Battle of Tsushima in the Russo-
Japanese War, and with less effectiveness at Jutland—is
"crossing the T." Utilizing superior speed or better
judgment, one commander may gradually bring his battle line across the enemy battle line at about a 90-degree
angle, thus crossing the "T" and bring the full weight
of broadside from his entire battle line to bear upon
the van of the enemy. The leading enemy ships, in such
a case, are almost certain to be sunk and his formation
disrupted.

Commerce warfare—the war of attrition—is quite a
different sort of thing from the climactic clash of two
great fleets.

The inferior power—and the United States is not

likely to be the inferior power in any war we may fight—
endeavors, in a war of attrition, to harass the enemy's
commerce, destroy as much of it as possible, and also
to reduce the strength of the enemy's fleet as much as
possible. He uses submarines and mines, planes when
possible, and surface commerce raiders, either cruisers,
pocket battleships, possibly battle cruisers, and armed
merchant cruisers. If the inferior power should happen
to be the United States we might even use a carrier
striking group, or a powerful fast-striking force composed of heavy cruisers or battle cruisers and possibly
a carrier, to smash suddenly against enemy commerce
lanes and coastline or against detachments of the enemy
fleet (probably the latter).

The answer to this type of warfare is convoy and
patrol—convoy on the surface and in the air. For the
United States this would mean careful guarding of
coastal convoys and of shipping to South America and
possibly to Australia and the Far East. Minesweepers,
working out of New York, San Francisco, and other
ports would daily sweep the bottlenecks of shipping;
submarine chasers; escort and convoy vessels and some
destroyers would probably accompany each convoy, as
would coastal blimps; and patrol planes would sweep
the waters ahead.

Convoys, to be effective, must be thoroughly guarded
from submarine, surface, and air attack. Preferably,
therefore, at least one cruiser should accompany each
convoy of twenty to fifty merchantmen; and destroyers
and other light craft should hover on flanks, in the van
and in the rear. Land-based planes or blimps can pro-

vide adequate aerial scouting as far as their range permits, but best protection against air attacks on convoys
can be given only by heavy antiaircraft equipment on
all the ships in the convoy and by fighting planes carried on an auxiliary carrier or regular naval carrier in
the convoy.

It is this latter type of warfare we are now called upon
to fight in the Atlantic. Merchant ships are being convoyed to Iceland; naval patrol plane bases have been
established at the Atlantic's focal points—Halifax, Newfoundland, Bermuda, and Iceland, Greenland, and else-
where. We are fighting a war of attrition, but we have
to fight it with weapons of Air Power as well as Sea
Power. The Atlantic strategy of such a war (unless
Britain should be eliminated from it) is essentially an
offensive strategy, in that our ships are being used to
assist in tightening the blockade around the Axis
powers, but on the other hand, many of our vessels are
used, in a tactical sense, defensively in convoy and
patrol work, etc.

In the Pacific, were we to fight Japan, both an offensive strategy and offensive tactics might be combined.
Certainly we would endeavor, insofar as possible, to
cut Japan's lines of communication to the outside world;
our submarines and surface raiders—perhaps a carrier-
striking group—would harry and sink Japanese commerce and strike at units of the Japanese Fleet.

The technique of a Pacific war has been much dis-
cussed; because of the vast distances of the greatest of
oceans it would be, at best, a difficult war, and one

which could not hope for a quick conclusion, even if
the United States were fighting in only one ocean. For,
as we have seen, if an enemy fleet does not wish to
accept the gauge of battle there is no way that the opposing fleet can make it do so; ships can stay safely in port
under protection of coastal fortifications and planes,
or can sortie out for brief raids, avoiding action when
they do so. The Japanese Fleet is inferior to our own
in strength; its mission should be to whittle down our
own Fleet by attrition attacks until the United States
Fleet were no longer superior in fighting strength.

Blockade of Japan from Hawaii and Singapore would
be an unprecedented task over an unprecedented distance, and probably could not alone be successful; certainly it would not force Japan to capitulate until the
slow effects of attrition had wasted her strength after
months and years of struggle. And such a blockade
could not even be instituted with much hope of success
unless there were a strong naval force—to back up the
blockade line—at Singapore, as well as at Hawaii.

Quicker results might be obtained by an even more
difficult strategy. We might attempt to send our Fleet
far into the Western Pacific, there to establish bases
and to clamp a close, rather than a distant blockade
around Japan, thus forcing her capitulation. There are
several routes to this end. One is the northern approach,
via Alaska and the Aleutians and the Japanese Kuriles,
a bleak, gale-tossed, and wind-swept route—possible,
but presenting gargantuan difficulties of distance and

climate and lack of adequate facilities. Another is a step-by-step advance—in which the Fleet Marine Force and the Army would play large roles—from Hawaii, Midway, and Wake westward towards Guam and beyond through the Japanese-mandated Islands. This would require precise and careful amphibian operations, the siege and seizure of outlying island bases, and the gradual consolidation of a chain of bases and a line of communications across the Pacific. Still another suggested course is a variation of this one—a step-by-step advance across the stepping stones of Pacific Islands further to the south in the general direction of the Philippines. And a fourth suggested alternative course of action, a course of daring, is the proposal that immediately upon the start of war, or before, our Fleet be despatched by a circuitous southern route, possibly via Australia, to Singapore, with a few advanced units based on Cavite.

Any or all of these courses of action would certainly lead to sea fights and epic struggles, but probably none of them would produce a general fleet engagement until after months or years of prefatory effort.

If at last the great fleets met, the history of nations would be written in the epic clash. . . .

Out of the dawn of the Western Pacific comes through the earphones a "contact" message—enemy fleet sighted. The blowers whine to full speed; the racing screws cut swaths of foam across the sea; on the flight decks of the carriers propellers turn in arcs of whirring light as the planes are readied. Below in the firerooms more burners are cut in as the needle on the steam gauge climbs.

The scouting forces clash; then comes the thundering meeting of the battle fleets. The planes roar up to the attack; patrol bombers from some island base fly like huge eagles of prey over the enemy battle line. Enemy planes zoom up to meet them, but down hurtle the sticks of bombs, and then, screeching out of the skies, drop the dive-bombers, and skimming across the wave tops roar the torpedo planes. Great spouts of water cascade into the sea—bomb splashes and shell splashes from the main batteries of the enemy battle line, used defensively against the torpedo planes. Hits are made, ships burst into flame, and now from the dim horizon our battle line thunders and our destroyers, at 30 knots, weave to the attack. The tracks of torpedoes line the sea; guns thunder; some stricken ship falls out of line and settles slowly behind the racing tide of battle. . . .

It is a scene of immense chaos and terrific power. But upon the outcome of some such struggle as this, or upon the slow pressure of the blockade, enforced by those dim distant ships which so few Americans ever see, may depend the dominion of the world.

GLOSSARY OF NAVAL AND NAUTICAL TERMS

ABAFT—Behind, or in the direction of, the stern.

ABEAM—On the beam of a vessel, or in a direction 90 degrees from the bow.

AHOY—A term used in hailing a vessel or small boat. Somewhat obsolescent.

AIGUILETTE—Gold and blue cord (for the Navy; gold and red for the Marine Corps and Army) worn from the left shoulder (right shoulder for Presidential aides) by all aides to senior officers.

ATHWARTSHIPS—Across ship, or at right angles to the fore-and-aft line.

AYE AYE, SIR—Response to an order, meaning, "The Order is understood, sir, and will be carried out."

BARBETTE—A cylinder of heavy armor extending from the lowest protective deck above the magazines to the armored turret and enclosing the turret foundation on which the rotating turret rests. The barbette is stationary.

BAROMETER—An instrument to measure atmospheric pressure.

BINNACLE—The stand in which the compass rests; in the old days the sick list used to be posted on the binnacle; hence the "binnacle list" today is the list of those under medical care.

BITTS—Wooden, iron, or steel cylindrical-shaped projections above the deck used for securing gear and making lines fast. Ropes, except in certain particular instances, are always called "lines" in the Navy, and they are always "made fast" or "belayed" instead of tied or fastened.

Bow—The forward part of the ship.

BROAD ON THE BOW—The direction or bearing of a ship or object 45 degrees from ahead.

BOAT—A ship is never a boat; it hurts the ears of a blue-jacket to hear his magnificent battleship referred to as a boat. Boats are small craft, carried by ships (lifeboats, sailboats, etc.). Slangily, destroyers and submarines are sometimes called "boats"; "in the boats" means you are serving in destroyers. But a destroyer sailor would be the first to think of his vessel as a SHIP with all the grandeur and dignity that that term implies to the nautical ear.

BULKHEAD—Transverse or longitudinal partitions (or walls) dividing the ship into compartments.

CAPSTAN—A vertical rotating barrel-like steel appliance, usually on modern ships located on the forecastle and used with the windlass for hauling in the anchor, and/or hauling upon lines, etc. In the old days it used to be man-powered; men manned capstan bars and walked the capstan round; now it is power-driven, though capstan bars are still available in case of power failure.

CASEMATE—Term usually applied to gun compartments along the side of a battleship. Gun casemates are no longer used on the modern battleships, but the term "casemate" can be understood as meaning a compartment aboard ship. Secondary batteries of battleships are now usually housed above the main deck in small turrets or gun housings.

CLAMP DOWN—To sprinkle and swab down the decks.

COAMING—The raised steel or wooden framework or "lip" about hatches or openings in the deck. Its purpose is to keep out water.

CONN—To direct the steering or course of a ship by giving orders to steersman (and to the engine room). The *conning tower,* heavily armored cylindrical structure of steel, with eye slits, is the captain's directing station during action.

DEAD RECKONING—Approximate position of a ship estimated by the navigator on the basis of courses steered and distances run without checking by observation of sun, stars, or moon. This is the deducted reckoning of the ship's position which was written as "DED" in old logs, hence the present use of "dead."

DOG WATCH—There are two Dog Watches; the first from 4 to 6 P.M., and the second from 6 to 8 P.M.

DRESSING SHIP—A display of flags or bunting rigged on "dressing lines" up over mastheads and to stem (bow) and stern on special occasions, such as the Fourth of July.

FATHOM—Six feet—a measure of depth.

FENDER—Wood, rope, canvas, or other substance used over the side of a ship to protect it from chafing when alongside a dock or another ship.

FIELD DAY—The Navy's term for a general ship (or station) cleaning. Usually every Friday.

FLOOR—The floors of a ship are properly termed "decks"; there are no floors in the ship's interior, though there are "floor plates"—removable iron plates in the fire (boiler) and engine rooms. "Floor," nautically used, is a term applied to the bottom, flat outside portion of the ship's hull. Also a floor is the athwartship member of the ship's frame tying the frames or ribs together and to the keel member.

FORECASTLE—In the old sailing days this was the crew's quarters forward in the ship and below decks. In the American Navy it is generally that portion of the ship's upper deck forward of the foremast. Officers' quarters in many American ships are forward rather than aft, thus reversing the ancient procedure.

FULL RUDDER—The rudder hard over. The rudder is a flat shape of steel or wood, pivoting on the stern post in the underwater rear of the ship and turned by power (steam or electricity). It steers the ship. The Navy's steering orders no longer use the terms "Starboard" (Right) or "Port" (Left) or the word "helm." The commands are "Right (or 'Left') Rudder," and the steering wheel, the rudder, and the bow of the ship all move to the right (or left).

GANGWAY—An opening in a ship's bulwarks or rails or side to permit entrance. A "gangway ladder" is an accommodation ladder or steep steps leading from a landing grating, alongside which boats may lie, to the gangway.

GROUND TACKLE—Anchor gear.

GYRO COMPASS—A compass whose axis is kept pointing to the true (not the magnetic) North by a rapidly spinning gyro, actuated electrically. Gyro compasses are now standard in Navy and magnetic compasses are used only as auxiliary or for check.

HEAVE THE LEAD—To take a sounding of the depth of the water with a heavy lead weight attached to a marked heaving line. A cavity in the end of the lead is sometimes "armed" with tallow for the purpose of bringing up a sample of the bottom.

HOLYSTONE—A large flat piece of sandstone used to clean and whiten a vessel's decks. Officially it is discountenanced in the modern Navy but is sometimes used nevertheless.

INTERNATIONAL RULES—Rules of the "road" governing the navigation of vessels under international agreement.

IRISH PENNANTS—Rope ends or loose ends hanging about a ship. A ship with Irish pennants flapping about is the opposite of shipshape.

JACKSTAFF—The flagstaff in the bow of a ship which carries the Union Jack. This is one way of telling whether a ship is at anchor, when seen from a distance. The Jack is flown from the jackstaff of a naval vessel only when the ship is anchored. The ensign or national colors are flown from the flagstaff aft, on the vessel's stern when anchored, and from the gaff or small spar abaft the mainmast when the ship is underway.

KEEL—The backbone of a ship; the steel members forming the bottom-most portion of a ship and from which the frames extend upward and outward. The keel is fixed rigidly to the stem in the bow and to the sternpost in the stern. The "bilge" is the curved part of the hull where the sides meet the bottom plating, and the "bilge keels" are metal fins or projections running longitudinally most of the length of the vessel and designed to dampen the vessel's roll.

KNOT—A knot is a measure of speed, and one should never say "knots per hour," for a knot is a nautical mile per hour, and to say "knots per hour" has no meaning and literally translated would be—"a nautical mile per hour per hour." A nautical mile is roughly 2,000 yards, or more exactly is one-sixtieth of a degree of latitude, and therefore varies with latitude from 6,046 feet to about 6,100 feet. But for all practical purposes a nautical mile is roughly equal to about 1.15 land or statute miles. A speed of 30 knots would roughly equal, therefore, a land speed of about 34½ miles per hour.

LADDER—All stairs aboard ship are called ladders.

LEEWARD—Direction away from the wind.

LIBERTY PARTY—A group of enlisted men entitled to, or on, shore leave. Usually the term is applied to brief absences from the ship, not to extended "vacations." Those who are entitled to long vacations are usually called "leave parties." "Lay aft the liberty (or leave) party" means in plain language, "Go to the after portion of the ship all those who are entitled to go ashore (or to go on vacation)."

LOG BOOK—The book in which is entered, watch by watch, the ship's history and record.

MAGAZINES—Compartments, usually at the very bottom of the ship, fireproof and kept at a constant temperature, where shells and powder are kept.

MARK—The markings on a lead line to show the depth of water in fathoms.

OFFICER OF THE DECK—Officer in charge of the watch and of the ship and on deck as the captain's representative.

PIPE DOWN—To pass the order to keep quiet. Or a shrill call blown on a boatswain's pipe dismissing the crew from a formation or drill. To "pipe the side" is a ceremony at which a boatswain's pipe is sounded when officer or other official boards or leaves the ship.

PLIMSOLL MARK—The mark, often painted in a circle on the outside of a merchant vessel's hull, which indicates the extreme loading draft.

QUARTER-DECK—Originally the after portion of a ship's deck, covering the captain's and officers' quarters. Now is usually aft, but any portion of a man-of-war's maindeck can now be designated as the quarter-deck and is usually reserved for official ceremonies, for greeting official visitors, and is the domain, in port, of the officer of the deck. The starboard side is traditionally reserved for the captain; the port for other officers.

RADIO COMPASS—A radio direction finder which takes the bearing or direction of a radio transmitting station and thus assists in determining the position of another ship or of your own ship in relation to the transmitting station.

RECOGNITION SIGNAL—An exchange of signals (secret in time of war) to disclose the identity of friendly vessels.

RUNNING LIGHTS—The lights carried by a vessel when underway. Warships and even merchant vessels do not carry lights in wartime.

SCUPPERS—Openings cut in ship's bulwarks or railing to permit deck water to run off. Usually fitted with scupper lips. Also sometimes used synonymously to mean the deck gutters or waterways around the sides of a deck.

SCUTTLE BUTT—A ship's drinking water fountain, or cask.

SEA COCK—A cock, or valve, in a connection opening to the sea; usually in the bottom of the ship; "to open the sea cocks" is to scuttle the vessel.

SHOVE OFF—To shove clear, push clear, get underway; leave (usually applied to small boats, leaving a dock).

SKIDS—Beams or cradles for the stowage of boats aboard ship.

SOUNDING—Measuring depth of the water, either with lead and line or by a sonic machine.

SPLICE THE MAIN BRACE—To have a drink.

SQUILGEE—A deck drier, flat piece of wood with rubber, and a handle.

STACK—The term used in the Navy for the smokestack or funnel of the ship.

STANCHION—A pillar or post aboard ship, a metal upright.

THWART—A seat running across, or at right angles to the length of, a boat.

TONNAGE—The size of naval ships is measured by *displacement;* that is the weight of the water actually displaced. Displacement varies with the quantity of stores aboard and the weight of the vessel. Standard displacement, by which naval vessels are compared, is the displacement of a vessel with stores, water, etc., aboard, but without oil.

Dead weight tonnage is the actual carrying capacity of a vessel, the weight of the load it can carry.

Gross tonnage is the entire internal capacity of a vessel, including machinery spaces, etc., measured in units of 100 cubic feet.

Net tonnage is the net internal capacity—cargo capacity—of a vessel measured in the cubic feet units, but deducting all machinery spaces, crew's quarters, etc., and all other spaces not available for passenger or freight carrying.

These latter three measures of a vessel's size are applied to cargo vessels or liners, not to men-of-war.

TRANSOM—A settee in a stateroom or messroom aboard ship.

UNDERWAY—Said of a ship when the ship is moving or drifting—when the ship is not moored to a dock or anchored. Often incorrectly spelled "Underweigh." The anchor is "a 'weigh," but the ship is never "underweigh."

WELL DECK—Usually the central portion of the main or upper deck, which is lower than the forward and after parts; hence "well" deck. Also applied sometimes, however, to the amidships portion—forward of the stacks, aft of the bridge—of the main deck of one of our flush-deck, four-stack destroyers.

WINDWARD—Direction from which the wind is blowing.

YARDARM BLINKERS—Signal lights on the signal yardarms of men-of-war actuated by a key on the signal bridge, used to send dash-and-dot messages by flashing light.

TABLES

THE following tables give a terse idea of the present strength and past growth of our Navy in ships and men, of the approximate costs of man-of-war construction, and of the distributions of those costs.

Full and complete data as to all elements of the Navy may be obtained, either from books listed in the following bibliography, or from reports of hearings before House and Senate Naval Affairs Committees, or from the annual reports of the Secretary of the Navy, the Chief of Naval Operations and the various chiefs of bureaus. These may be consulted at a public library or procured from Congress, the Government Printing Office, or the Navy Department in Washington.

TABLE I

GROWTH OF THE NAVY

ENLISTED MEN

	NAVY	MARINE CORPS
June 30, 1933	79,243	14,876
June 30, 1934	80,359	15,174
June 30, 1935	82,839	16,097
June 30, 1936	93,077	16,040
June 30, 1937	100,180	16,911
June 30, 1938	104,888	16,997
June 30, 1939	110,196	18,013
May 23, 1940	136,164	25,045
October 1, 1941	219,165	47,027

TABLE II

MAJOR NAVIES OF THE WORLD

COMBATANT SHIPS, BUILT AND BUILDING
(JANUARY 1941)
(ALL FIGURES ESTIMATES ONLY)

TYPE	BUILT	BUILDING	TOTAL
UNITED STATES			
Battleships	15	17	32
Aircraft Carriers ...	6	12	18
Cruisers	37	54	91
Destroyers	159	205	364
Submarines	105	80	185
TOTAL	322	368	690
BRITISH EMPIRE			
Battleships	16	7	23
Aircraft Carriers ...	7	5	12
Cruisers	62	21	83
Destroyers	221	18	239
Submarines	52	4	56
TOTAL	358	55	413
JAPAN			
Battleships	10	4	14
Aircraft Carriers ...	4	2	6
Cruisers	44	6	50
Destroyers	135	11	146
Submarines	69	13	82
TOTAL	262	36	298

TYPE	BUILT	BUILDING	TOTAL
FRANCE			
Battleships	1	4 ?	5
Aircraft Carriers ..	1	2	3
Cruisers	14	3	17
Destroyers	52	30	82
Submarines	60	25	85
TOTAL	128	64 ?	192 ?
ITALY			
Battleships	6	2	8
Aircraft Carriers ...	0	0	0
Cruisers	20	14	34
Destroyers	120	12	132
Submarines	94	21	115
TOTAL	240	49	289
GERMANY			
Battleships	6	2	8
Aircraft Carriers ...	1	1	2
Cruisers	7	6	13
Destroyers	47	?	47 ?
Submarines	120 ?	180 ?	300
TOTAL	181	189	370 ?
RUSSIA			
Battleships	3	0	3
Aircraft Carriers ...	1	2 ?	3 ?
Cruisers	9	4	13
Destroyers	67	16 ?	83 ?
Submarines	171 ?	?	171 ?
TOTAL	251	22 ?	273 ?

(No deductions made for ships *damaged* in war)

Table III

Approximate Distribution of Estimated Costs of Naval Vessels

Approximate Total Costs Covering Construction, Hull, Machinery, Armor, Armament, and Ammunition

VESSEL	APPROXIMATE ESTIMATE	LABOR AT SITE	LABOR AWAY FROM SITE	COST OF RAW MATERIALS
Battleship	$70,850,300	$35,000,000	$25,223,300	$10,627,000
Cruiser	22,300,000	11,000,000	7,950,000	3,350,000
Aircraft carrier	31,600,000	15,800,000	11,130,000	4,670,000
Destroyer	8,000,000	4,000,000	3,200,000	1,300,000
Submarine	6,500,000	3,000,000	2,500,000	1,000,000
Submarine tender	12,600,000	6,500,000	5,200,000	1,900,000
Seaplane tender	13,000,000	6,500,000	4,550,000	1,950,000
Destroyer tender	13,000,000	6,500,000	4,550,000	1,950,000
Oiler	6,000,000	3,000,000	2,100,000	900,000
Minesweeper	2,500,000	1,250,000	875,000	375,000
Fleet tug	2,000,000	1,000,000	700,000	300,000

Table IV

Prepared in the Bureau of Labor Statistics Division of Construction and Public Employment U. S. Department of Labor

An Estimate of the Effect of $1,000,000 of Construction—Contracts Awarded for Naval Vessel Construction *

Expenditures for:

Labor	$391,000	39.1%
Material	406,000	40.6%
Other expenses and profit	203,000	20.3%

Man-hours worked:

    At the construction site 491,000
    In mines, factories, transportation, and in
       administration 589,000

Value of material orders placed:

ALL MATERIALS $406,000
    Aluminum sheets, shapes, and castings.. 2,000
    Boilers 10,000
    Bolts, nuts, washers, and rivets........ 3,000
    Electrical machinery apparatus and sup-
       plies 52,000
    Electric wiring and fixtures............ 24,000
    Elevators and elevator equipment...... 4,000
    Engines, turbines, auxiliary machinery
       and equipment 47,000
    Forgings, iron and steel.............. 10,000
    Foundry and machine-shop products, not
       elsewhere classified 56,000
    Furniture and furnishings 4,000
    Hardware, miscellaneous 1,000
    Heating and ventilating equipment..... 6,000
    Instruments 2,000
    Lumber 2,000
    Machine tools 2,000
    Metal doors, shutters, molding and trim. 4,000
    Non-ferrous metal castings, sheets, pipe
       and tubing, etc., n.e.c. 26,000
    Paints and varnishes 3,000
    Petroleum products 5,000

Plumbing fixtures and supplies	1,000
Pumps and pumping equipment	12,000
Steel-works and rolling-mill products, not elsewhere classified	90,000
Wall plaster, wall board, and insulation material	2,000
Wire and wireworks products	5,000
Other materials	33,000

* Estimate based on a study made of the construction costs of the following naval vessels constructed in private shipyards: Ten destroyers, two submarines, two aircraft carriers, two light cruisers, and one heavy cruiser.

NAVAL BIBLIOGRAPHY

FOR those nautically inclined landsmen who desire a closer acquaintance with the Navy and things of the Navy than the scope of this book permits, the following list of books is appended. This is by no means an exhaustive list; works about the Navy occupy scores of shelves in every library in the country. But it is a typical one, and all of the books listed have been consulted in the preparation of this book. So the author acknowledges a debt of gratitude to the authors of these more specialized works and hopes that he may repay it by earnestly suggesting to readers, avid after knowledge of our first line of defense, that they can do no better than to consult some, or all, of these books.

SEA POWER—GENERAL: ITS ELEMENTS AND ITS USES
Sea Power and the Modern World. Admiral Sir Herbert Richmond. Reynal and Hitchcock.
The Influence of Sea Power Upon History. Captain A. T. Mahan. Little, Brown and Co.
Sea Power and Today's War. Fletcher Pratt. Harrison-Hilton.

UNITED STATES NAVY—GENERAL
The United States Navy. Senate Document No. 35, 75th Congress, 1st Session. Superintendent of Documents, Government Printing Office, Washington, D. C.

CR

CRITICAL

The United States Navy in Peacetime. Government Printing Office, Washington, D. C.

The United States Navy. Merle Armitage. Longmans, Green and Co.

World Almanac

Encyclopaedia Britannica

UNITED STATES NAVAL HISTORY

A History of the United States Navy. Captain Dudley W. Knox. Putnam.

NAVAL POLICY

The Rise of American Naval Power

Toward a New Order of Sea Power. Harold and Margaret Sprout. Princeton University Press.

NAVAL TRADITIONS AND EARLY HISTORY

Naval Traditions, Customs and Usage. Lieutenant Commander Leland P. Lovette. U. S. Naval Institute, Annapolis.

Room to Swing a Cat. Lieutenant F. J. Bell. Longmans, Green and Co.

Education in the Early Navy. Henry L. Burr. Dissertation submitted to Temple University, Philadelphia.

THE ENLISTED MAN

The Bluejacket's Manual—1940. U. S. Naval Institute, Annapolis, Maryland.

The Fleet Today. Kendall Banning. Funk and Wagnalls Co.

THE OFFICER

Annapolis Today. Kendall Banning. Funk and Wagnalls Co.

Naval Rank. Chief Gunner Lawrence Fasano. Horizon House.

THE FIGHTING SHIPS—WORLD

Jane's Fighting Ships—1940. Sampson Low, Marston and Co., Ltd., London.

Weyers Taschenbuch der Kriegsflotten, in German, but a far more handy, pocket-size reference book than the bulky Jane's. 1940. J. F. Lehmanns Verlag, Munich, Germany.

U. S. FIGHTING SHIPS

The Ships and Aircraft of the U. S. Fleet. James C. Fahey. Herald-Nathan Press, 460 West 34th Street, New York.

Ship's Data, U. S. Naval Vessels. Government Printing Office, Washington, D. C.

THE FIGHTING PLANES—WORLD

Jane's All the World's Aircraft. Sampson Low, Marston and Co., Ltd., London.

THE FIGHTING PLANES—UNITED STATES

The Ships and Aircraft of the U. S. Fleet. Fahey, *ibid.*

Aviation (a magazine). Annual Directory Number, February, 1940, McGraw-Hill Publishing Company, New York.

EQUIPMENT

Naval Ordnance, U. S. Naval Institute, Annapolis, Maryland.

Mine and Countermine. A. M. Low. Sheridan House, New York.

SHIPBUILDING AND CONSTRUCTION
Modern Shipfitter's Handbook. W. E. Swanson. Cornell Maritime Press, New York.

SEAMANSHIP
Modern Seamanship. Rear Admiral Austin M. Knight. D. Van Nostrand Co., New York.

BASES
Navy Directory. U. S. Government Printing Office, Washington, D. C. Senate Document No. 35, *ibid.*

THE FLEET
War in the Pacific. Denlinger and Gary. McBride, New York.

USE OF THE FLEET
War in the Pacific. Ibid.
The Great Pacific War. Hector C. Bywater. Houghton Mifflin Co., New York.

THE NAVY AS AN ELEMENT OF OUR DEFENSE
United We Stand. Hanson W. Baldwin. Whittlesey House, New York.
If War Comes. Dupuy and Eliot. Macmillan, New York.
The Ramparts We Watch. Major George Fielding Eliot. Reynal and Hitchcock, New York.

NAVAL AND NAUTICAL NOMENCLATURE
Naval Terms and Definitions. Commander C. C. Soule. D. Van Nostrand Co., New York.
A Dictionary of Sea Terms. A. Ansted. Brown, Son and Ferguson, Ltd., Glasgow, Scotland.

INDEX